Scotland
FROM THE AIR

TEXT BY GILES GORDON
PHOTOGRAPHY BY JASON HAWKES

TED SMART

Contents

Introduction

Introduction

TAYSIDE

This picture suggests that Cézanne might have painted Tayside. It is one of the loveliest areas of Scotland, embracing within its purlieus the cities of Dundee and Perth; Arbroath (as in 'smokies') and golfing St Andrews; Loch Leven (on whose island Mary, Queen of Scots was imprisoned) and Anstruther; Gleneagles (as in golf and hotel); Blair Castle and Blair Atholl; Glamis Castle (as in the Scots play by Shakespeare, the home of the Queen Mother during her childhood and Princess Margaret's birthplace) and Brechin.

Who would surmise any of this scenario from these gentle, well-manicured fields and quietly rolling forest-clad hills?

It is a commonplace that books such as this – bought for their pretty, even spectacular and thoroughly sophisticated photographs – are bolstered up with undemanding texts which sketch, in as few words as possible, the history of the country. Employing as unpurplish a prose as possible to colour the landscape, such texts comment on the achievements of the nation and generally do an efficient, sycophantic PR job.

This book does not comprise pretty views (*à la* Colin Baxter) in the sense that most picture books of Scotland do; Scotland, not least the Highlands, presenting a picturesque landscape. The only picture of heather is of heather burning. There are no pictures of pipers; of men or, more yuckily, girls in kilts; of whisky being drunk or haggis being eaten; of Highland games (brawny giants tossing, if that is the word, phallic-shaped tree trunks) or of fishermen idling their lives away, and only occasionally capturing their tea, by the shores of loch or river. There are no footballers or golfers, or even curlers; and if there are seals and sea birds they are viewed from a distance. There are no ancient crones garbed in black, or ridiculously bewhiskered old buffers; no soldiers in uniform; no deer stalkers (or deerstalkers, the hats rather than the chaps), although there is a lovely shot of red deer. There are no poses of members of the Royal Company of Archers, of the Lord Lyon King of Arms or of the Moderator of the Church of Scotland or of Scotland's Cardinal, the latter pair respectively garbed in blackest of black and reddest of red. There are not even pictures of Her Majesty the Queen and other members of the Royal Family decanting themselves with smiles from Crathie parish church after Sunday service.

Jason Hawkes, with his pilot Tim Kendall, climbed into his helicopter to take stunning pictures from the air which give a new perspective to often familiar sights. What he has come up with is a pattern of Scotland, an aesthetic of landscape – and seascape, for to Scotland the coast and the water are as essential as the land – more evocative and imaginative, certainly fresher, than most such collections of photographs.

Scotland may be a small country – the land mass is just over 30,000 square miles; from the southernmost point to the most northern tip is 274 miles; and it is approximately 154 miles across – but it takes itself, we take ourselves, desperately seriously. No people is prouder, and prouder of its country and heritage. In 'Resolution and Independence', Wordsworth wrote of:

Choice words, and measured phrase, above the reach of ordinary men. A stately speech; Such as great livers do in Scotland use.

He was not, I take it, speaking of the effect on one of the body's vital organs after imbibing too many drams of the country's national beverage.

The Scots, who pride themselves both on their education and their educational system, have a marvellous sense of history; their history, albeit too frequently seen through a romantic hue. Even the most solemn Protestants betray a twinge of nostalgia, of what might have been, when the Jacobite rebellions are mentioned, especially that of 1745 and the egregious Charles Edward Stewart, better known as Bonnie Prince Charlie. Recently, thanks to a duo of mainly American-financed films, Scotland's bloody Wars of Independence with and versus the English (1297–1304 and 1306–28) have again been exciting the Scottish blood, and the ever-hopeful Scottish National Party has been trying to cash in on the films' sentiments and commercial success.

The first film was about Rob Roy MacGregor (1671–1734), starring the Irish actor Liam Neeson; it was at least filmed in Scotland and the scenery looks wonderful. The second film portrayed William Wallace (1274–1305) with Australian actor Mel Gibson (of course he claimed Scottish antecedents; who doesn't?) essaying the life of the thirteenth-century patriot. This film, *Braveheart*, was made by a Hollywood studio and the bogs of Ireland were used as a stand-in for the braes of Scotland. Why? Because there are tax breaks for film makers in Ireland.

Gibson went on record after the film's premiere in Stirling, condemning the SNP for hijacking his movie to promote a big recruitment drive. 'I didn't make the film for any kind of political use like that at all,' he said. 'It shouldn't be used as a tool for political gain or loss.' A spokesman for the SNP responded: 'We

'I pluck these names from my head, late at night. Tomorrow morning could provide an equally impressive, different list . . . . For a nation its size, Scotland's achievement is prodigious. '

admit it's cheeky but then so was Wallace. We want to capitalize on the movie.'

Michael Forsyth, the Secretary of State for Scotland in the Conservative administration in London, turned up for the premiere wearing a kilt. 'It's a film about fighting injustice and intolerance and I think the people of Scotland want to fight the battles of the twenty-first century, which are about jobs and prosperity, not the battles of the fourteenth century. I think it shows the irrelevance of the SNP to the real issues.' He would say that, wouldn't he?

Forsyth's opposite number in the Labour Party, George Robertson, opined of the film: 'It will do much for the Scottish Tourist Board, but nothing for the SNP. The people of Scotland are not stupid, nor are they a downtrodden race.' Indeed not, sir.

Please come back, Sean Connery. Even your worst films, and they are not necessarily *Highlander* and *Highlander II*, make us proud to be Scots; and there's no need for you to buy a new set of teeth. The sibilant sounds your one-time Edinburgh milkman's voice make with the language are as essential as any malt.

The history that Scots, higher-educated or self-educated, tend to summon up is anecdotal, biographical; mainly about men, occasionally about women. There are Columba and Margaret, saints both; Wallace and Bruce; Old and Young Pretenders to the throne, James Edward Stewart and his grandson, Charles Edward Stewart; Flora MacDonald and Jenny Geddes; Mary, Queen of Scots and John Knox, hero to some, villain to others, bore to more; the Renaissance kings, James IV and James V; and James VI and I, dispatched with his tobacco and homosexuality to London in 1603 when Mary's great rival, Elizabeth, died.

There are writers: Walter Scott, Rabbie Burns, Robert Louis Stevenson, J. M. Barrie and Hugh MacDiarmid. (It was Barrie, dreamer of *Peter Pan*, who wrote in another play, *What Every Woman Knows*: 'There are few more impressive sights in the world than a Scotsman on the make.' And later in the same play: 'You've forgotten the grandest moral attribute of a Scotsman, Maggie, that he'll do nothing which might damage his career.')

There are painters: Allan Ramsay, Henry Raeburn, David Wilkie, William McTaggart, the Colourists. There is David Hume, philosopher *par excellence*, and Adam Smith, economist ditto. Mungo Park and David Livingstone, explorers. William Adam and his son Robert Adam, W. H. Playfair, Alexander 'Greek' Thomson and Charles Rennie Mackintosh, architects. James Watt, James Young Simpson, Alexander Graham Bell and John Logie Baird, inventors. James Clerk Maxwell, scientist. James Boswell, foil to Dr Johnson. Henry Dundas, Viscount Melville and Ramsay MacDonald, politicians. Andrew Carnegie, philanthopist, and Patrick Geddes, polymath. Douglas Haig, soldier, and Lord Reith, creator of the BBC. Harry Lauder and Billy Connolly, comedians.

I pluck these names from my head, late at night. Tomorrow morning could provide an equally impressive, different list. (It might include Macbeth, David I, Thomas the Rhymer, George Buchanan, John Napier, Thomas Telford, Lord Braxfield, Joseph Lister, Francis Jeffrey, Thomas Carlyle, James Hogg, Lord Cockburn, Lord Byron, Deacon Brodie, John McAdam, Compton Mackenzie, Eric Liddell, and on and on.) For a nation its size, Scotland's achievement is prodigious.

Irony and education, or education and irony, are the country's staple commodities. In post-Thatcher Britain (Scotland at the time of writing returns but ten Conservative MPs to Westminster), homeless young men and women offer for sale *The Big Issue* on many of Edinburgh's thoroughfares throughout the day. This is a worthy means by which the homeless may hope to make some money.

There are also, as in Glasgow, beggars galore. The other day I was proceeding up the Playfair Steps from Princes Street past the Royal Scottish Academy and the National Gallery to Market Street to meet someone for lunch at the agreeable Doric Tavern. A beggar requested some change. My thoughts were elsewhere, and I didn't pause in my progress. I shook my head, and looked him in the eye, apologizing. 'Don't look so glum,' he said. 'I'm sure your worries are far worse than mine.' He was, I suppose, being ironic. That is what makes Scotland such a quirky and stimulating country in which to live, and, of course, to visit.

The Union of the Crowns of England and Scotland happened because England, with the death of the childless Elizabeth, had no legitimate, or indeed any, heir acceptable to all. Admittedly, this was not usually an encumbrance to an ambitious person desirous of becoming monarch. Just over a century later, in 1707, was enacted the Treaty of Union, intended to cement the parliaments and governments of the two countries.

Scotland's history until then (let us leave England to fend for itself) had not predicated that such a union was either necessary or appropriate. Internecine warfare between the two countries had, through the centuries, been both ferocious and fatuous. Scotland had won at Bannockburn (1314) but had lost at Flodden (1513). The Calvinist Reformation of John Knox prospered in the 1560s, but the Jacobites (1689–1746) lost their Risings in much the same way, but with infinitely more bloodshed, that the Scottish National Party keeps being denied power.

Yet if considered in terms of heroes and heroines, or even Hollywood – and there *are* more misleading yardsticks – Scotland's history is undoubtedly romantic.

Here are some key events: the Romans consolidated positions in Scotland from AD 81–350. In 367 the Picts, Scots and Saxons attacked the Romans, but a couple of years later the Barbarians were quelled and Roman authority re-established. The Picts were defeated in battle by the Romans under Magnus Maximus in 382, but in 401 the Roman legions began to leave Britain, allowing local tribes to reassert themselves. In 563 St Columba established (hence, in a manner of speaking, the Church of Scotland becoming the country's Established Church in 1690) a Celtic church on Iona, today unfortunately one of the more saccharine islands, too much visited. Around 1034 the Scottish tribes were for the first time united, under Duncan I. This perhaps gave Shakespeare the wrong idea that the king was a wise and elderly greybeard and Macbeth an evil upstart, rather than vice versa. In 1263 Alexander II stymied King Haakon of Norway, who thought he had a right to the throne

of Scotland, at the Battle of Largs, thus ending Norse domination of the Hebrides.

At the end of the thirteenth century (1297) William Wallace was inspired to lead a resistance movement against Edward I, 'The Hammer of the Scots', and the English army. Wallace was routed at the Battle of Falkirk (1298) and later betrayed (the Christ parallel has fed the myth) to the English by Sir John de Menteith, a covetous Scot. Wallace was dragged to London, tried for treason – a trumped-up charge if ever there was one, as he had never acknowledged English supremacy in Scotland – and hanged, drawn and quartered. The quarters were distributed to Perth, Berwick, Stirling and Newcastle, to discourage others.

His life had in no sense been lived in vain as it spurred on Robert the Bruce to pick up the gauntlet, or fly the saltire, and crush the English at the Battle of Bannockburn (1314). Six years later in 1320, the Declaration of Arbroath, directed against Pope John XXII, asserted Scotland's independence; not from Rome but from England.

The year 1371, not a significant date in itself, saw the accession to the throne of Robert II, grandson of Robert the Bruce, and the first Stewart king, an event which had repercussions down the centuries. In 1503 the 'glittering and tragic king' James IV, Scotland's renaissance prince, married Margaret Tudor, daughter of Henry VII. In 1513 he was cut down in the Borders at the Battle of Flodden, inspiring Jean Elliot (1727–1805) to write 'The Flowers of the Forest' published in Herd's *Scottish Songs* (1776), the last two stanzas of which read:

> Dule* and wae for the order sent our
>   lads to the Border;
> The English, for ance, by guile wan the day;
> The Flowers of the Forest, that fought aye
>   the foremost,
> The prime o' our land, are cauld in the clay.
> We'll hear nae mair lilting at yowe-milking,
> Women and bairns are heartless and wae;
> Sighing and moaning on ilka green loaning:*
> The Flowers of the Forest are a' wede away.

> *dule: grief   *loaning: a milking-park

> *'If considered in terms of heroes and heroines, or even Hollywood – and there* are *more misleading yardsticks – Scotland's history is undoubtedly romantic.'*

11

NORTH MONADHLIATH MOUNTAINS

Geologically, the Highland landscape comprises a dissected plateau of crystalline rocks made into glens and lochs by the ancient action of ice and mountain. The end result – the Highlands today – is a wide area of irregularly distributed mountain ranges: Cairngorm, Grampian and Monadhliath. Monadhliath runs north-east from Lochaber, dividing Speyside and Badenoch from the Great Glen. Monadhliath means 'Grey Mountains', and they are, it has to be said, not the liveliest of the country's peaks.

The mountains are inhabited by grouse and ptarmigan, red deer and roe, and forestry. General Wade's military road, seen to the top right of the picture, made use of the Corrieyairack Pass. Bonnie Prince Charlie took to the road as he advanced in 1745; and it was back into the Monadhliath Mountains that he fled after his defeat at Culloden.

1560 saw the Reformation and the serious rise of serious John Knox. In 1587 Mary, Queen of Scots, after much jiggery-popery posing as politics, had her head divided from her, by all accounts, spectacular neck. This indirectly, but probably inevitably given the brutes around, led to the 1603 Union of the Crowns.

1638–66 saw the Covenanters defending Presbyterianism and Scottish communicants' rights to deal direct with God and not through the English king, priest confessors and 'all kinds of Papistry'. 1689 witnessed the first Jacobite rebellion to oust the Protestant bed-wedded monarchs, William and Mary, and to restore the Stewarts and Roman Catholicism to Scotland, crushed at the Battle of Killiecrankie after the death of its leader, James Graham of Claverhouse.

1692 was the year of the terrible, dark massacre of Glencoe, the Sharpeville of its time, a relatively trivial event which history would blow up – but not out of proportion – to suggest, rightly, a malaise in the kingdom, something rotten in the state of Scotland.

The Union of Scotland and England, at least as far as the English were and are concerned, translated the two countries into a new amalgam, Great Britain. 1715 saw the Highlanders trying to make James VII and II's son, James Edward Stewart (1688–1766), 'The Old Pretender', into King James VIII. Thirty years later there was a kind of action replay with James Edward Stewart's son, Charles Edward Stewart (1720–88), 'The Young Pretender', raising, rousing and carousing the clans once more. Initially they thrashed the Hanoverians, headily deciding to march upon London and being, for better or for worse, obliterated at Culloden Moor, near Inverness in 1746.

It is not cricket (an English game) to point out that more Scots fought at Culloden for the English, mainly Protestant, army under William Augustus, Duke of Cumberland ('Butcher' to his enemies), than for the be-frilled and Frenchified Bonnie Prince Charlie. The battle led directly to the forced breakup of the clan system (with the banning of spoken Gaelic, wearing tartan, playing bagpipes and carrying weapons) and to the Highland Clearances, whereby sheep were cynically preferred to men, women and bairns.

King George IV's state visit to Scotland in 1822 saw the fat-legged Hanoverian monarch sporting the kilt, and was in a way the last indigenous Scottish event in the Simple History annals. After that, the world became greyer, with Scotland playing its part on the international stage.

Scotland's scientists and engineers played a great part in the Industrial Revolution, and in its aftermath. There was ever a tendency, not least when Victoria was on the throne, for Scots to seek their fortunes overseas. Scottish soldiers and explorers did their bit to see that as much of the globe as possible was painted tartan. Historian Michael Fry's next book will be called *The Scottish Empire*, and he takes that to be most of the planet, including the American continent, India, Africa and Australia. Scots were eager too in the mission field. (I've always thought the journalist H. M. Stanley meant to say, when encountering the great David Livingstone by Lake Tanganyika in 1871, 'Dr Livingstone, you presume!' Whatever, Stanley's account of Livingstone's struggle to make slave owners understand the iniquity of their trade makes him one of the great Scottish heroes.

We've had our share of famous events, inventions and discoveries, outstanding men and women. But what of Scotland as a whole, the generality of the population? The most recent census was in April 1991. The country's population was just under five million – London's population at the time was seven million. Glasgow had 654,000 citizens (100,000 down on ten years earlier); Edinburgh 422,000; Aberdeen 201,000; and Dundee 166,000; these being the four largest cities (and each having a Lord Provost).

What occupations do the Scots espouse? They have been, and continue to be, explorers, divines and soldiers; engineers, scientists and inventors; lawyers, bankers and accountants; doctors and teachers; architects, writers and artists. These are the Scottish professions; which is not, of course, to assert that all Scots follow them, only that in these directions preferment and privilege frequently lie. The Scots, unlike the English and those settling here from the uncertainties of the Indian subcontinent, are most emphatically not a nation of shopkeepers.

Too often, at least in the past, it seemed that the Scots were not a nation of hoteliers or restaurateurs either. But today Edinburgh and Glasgow possess some of the classiest restaurants in Europe. Some of the hotels, particularly outside the cities and excluding the hydros (which have swimming pools and are usually good value), are fairly grim places and outrageously expensive. The Scottish Tourist Board, founded in 1945, still has quite a way to go in making the Scottish tourist industry understand that visitors expect first-class service and fare these days.

If you are a visitor to our beautiful country, whether the Highlands and Islands or the Lowlands, enjoy Scotland's incomparable variety and Jason Hawkes' uplifting photographs. If you are a native or resident in the country, you will see it differently from before as a result of studying these thrilling pictures.

Breathes there the man with soul so dead,
Who never to himself hath said,
This is my own, my native land!
Whose heart hath ne'er within him burned,
As home his footsteps he hath turned
From wandering on a foreign strand?
O Caledonia! stern and wild,
Meet nurse for a poetic child!
Land of brown heath and shaggy wood,
Land of the mountain and the flood,
Land of my sires!

The Lay of the Last Minstrel (1805)
Sir Walter Scott (1771–1832)

13

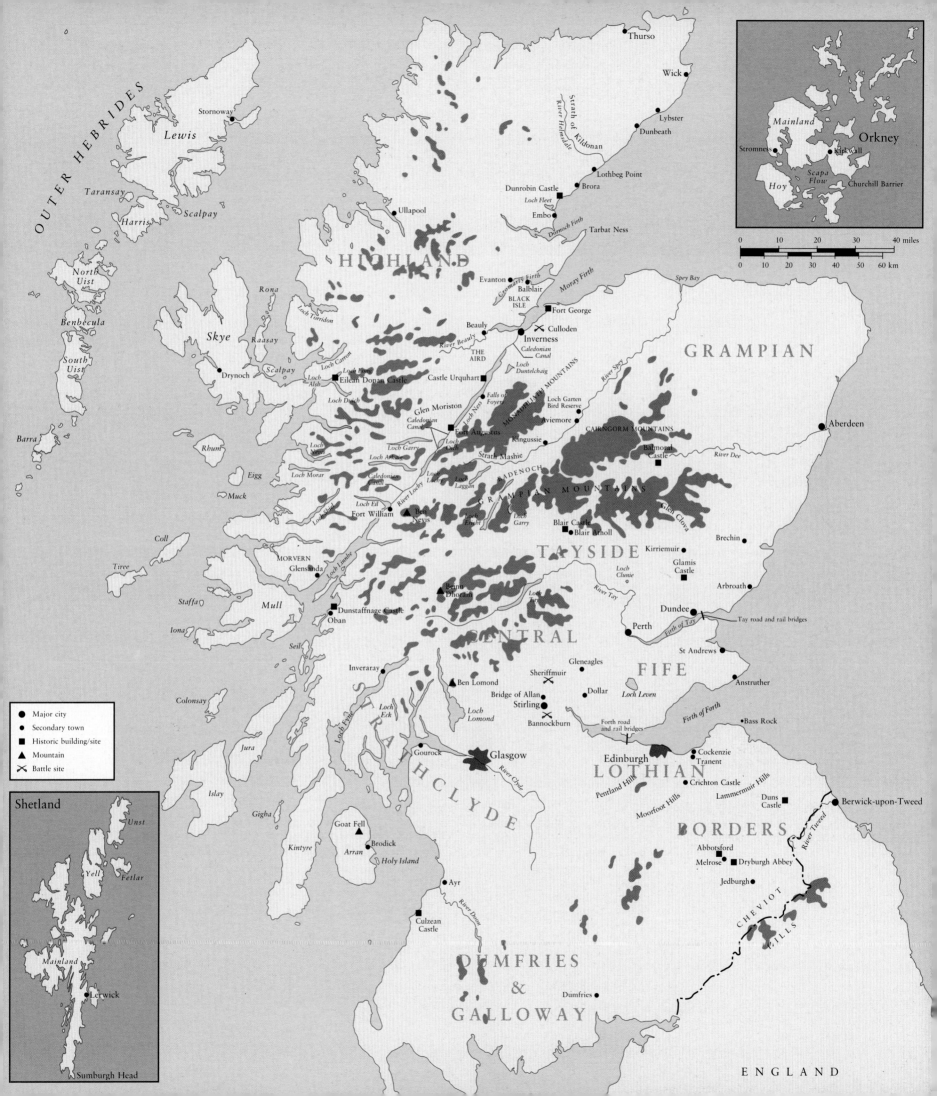

OUTER HEBRIDES

Lewis

Stornoway

Taransay

Scalpay

Harris

North Uist

Rona

Benbécula

Skye

Raasay

South Uist

Drynoch

Scalpay

Barra

Rhum

Eigg

Muck

Coll

Tiree

Staffa

Iona

Mull

Seil

Colonsay

Jura

Islay

Gigha

Kintyre

Arran

Goat Fell

Brodick

Holy Island

Thurso

Wick

Lybster

Dunbeath

Strath of Kildonan

River Helmsdale

Lothbeg Point

Brora

Dunrobin Castle

Loch Fleet

Embo

Dornoch Firth

Tarbat Ness

Ullapool

HIGHLAND

Evanton

Cromarty Firth

Balblair

Moray Firth

Spey Bay

BLACK ISLE

Fort George

Beauly

Culloden

Inverness

River Beauly

THE AIRD

Caledonian Canal

Loch Duntelchaig

GRAMPIAN

Loch Torridon

Loch Carron

Eilean Donan Castle

Castle Urquhart

Loch Long

Loch Alsh

Loch Duich

Glen Moriston

Falls of Foyers

Aberdeen

Loch Garten Bird Reserve

MONADHLIATH MOUNTAINS

Aviemore

Caledonian Canal

Loch Ness

Fort Augustus

Kingussie

Loch Oich

Strath Mashie

CAIRNGORM MOUNTAINS

Balmoral Castle

Loch Garry

Loch Ness

BADENOCH

River Dee

Loch Arkaig

Loch Lochy

Loch Laggan

GRAMPIAN MOUNTAINS

Caledonian Canal

Loch Eil

River Lochy

Fort William

Ben Nevis

Loch Eil

Loch Eight

Loch Garry

Blair Castle

Blair Atholl

Glen Clova

Loch Shiel

Loch Linnhe

MORVERN

Glensanda

Beinn Dhorain

Brechin

TAYSIDE

Kirriemuir

Glamis Castle

Loch Clunie

Arbroath

Dunstaffnage Castle

Oban

Loch Tay

River Tay

Dundee

Firth of Tay

Tay road and rail bridges

Perth

St Andrews

CENTRAL

Inveraray

Loch Fyne

Loch Eck

Ben Lomond

FIFE

Gleneagles

Sheriffmuir

Anstruther

Bridge of Allan

Dollar

Loch Leven

Stirling

Loch Lomond

Bannockburn

Firth of Forth

Forth road and rail bridges

Bass Rock

STRATHCLYDE

Gourock

Glasgow

River Clyde

Edinburgh

Cockenzie

Tranent

LOTHIAN

Crichton Castle

Pentland Hills

Moorfoot Hills

Lammermuir Hills

Duns Castle

Berwick-upon-Tweed

BORDERS

Abbotsford

River Tweed

Melrose

Dryburgh Abbey

Jedburgh

CHEVIOT HILLS

Ayr

River Doon

Culzean Castle

DUMFRIES & GALLOWAY

Dumfries

ENGLAND

Legend

- ● Major city
- • Secondary town
- ■ Historic building/site
- ▲ Mountain
- ✕ Battle site

Orkney (inset)

Mainland

Orkney

Stromness

Kirkwall

Hoy

Scapa Flow

Churchill Barrier

0   10   20   30   40 miles

0   10   20   30   40   50   60 km

Shetland (inset)

Unst

Yell

Fetlar

Mainland

Lerwick

Sumburgh Head

Borders

THE BORDERS

Who would surmise, encountering this view, that for centuries it was the site of much bloodshed? These quiet fields keep discreet and wary watch over England. The Borders are, essentially, and were historically, the border between Scotland and England, a border which shifted north or south subject to fluctuations in power between the two neighbours. Thus Berwick-upon-Tweed was sometimes English, sometimes Scottish. It is now the most northern town in England.

The division between the two countries is marked by the River Tweed and the Cheviot Hills. This gentle, unassuming countryside, so unlike that of the Highlands, has down the centuries seen far too much blood spilt, often that of Scots by Scots. The most famous of the lawless, anarchic Border reivers – robbers and freebooters, adept at stealing each other's cattle – was Johnnie Armstrong, hanged in 1529 alongside thirty-six of his gang by the seventeen-year-old King James V.

Today, the Borders get on with life, much taken as they are with market towns, farming, riding, rugby and fishing. Their tumultuous past allows them to enjoy a peaceful present.

TOWARDS THE MOORFOOT HILLS

One of the pleasures of living in Scotland is the opportunity for walking in the countryside and in the hills. Walks around Edinburgh are particularly pleasurable. South of the capital are three main groups of hills: to the west, the Pentlands; to the east, the Lammermuirs; and in the centre, the Moorfoots. This photograph shows the landscape looking east from the A703 south of Edinburgh and towards the Moorfoot Hills.

These days public transport is so inadequate that, if you're not to be exhausted before you begin walking seriously, you should make for the start of your walk by car. John Chalmers and Derek Storey in their *One Hundred Hill Walks Around Edinburgh* give details of eleven walks in the Moorfoots, none of them more than 25 miles from the city. Some walks, obviously, are more arduous than others, and they take in a variety of scenery, including heather-covered moorlands, peat bogs, drainage ditches,

grazing land and grass tussocks, good firm paths and forested mountain glens. Yes, at times the ground can be squelchy underfoot. There are, constantly, invigorating panoramic views including vistas of the Firth of Forth and Midlothian.

FORESTRY IN THE BORDERS

I wish the chopped-down conifers depicted here presaged a *Cherry Orchard*-like destruction; but not that the firs should be replaced by cheap, or council, housing. Christmas trees, seen singly and twinkling with fairy lights, are fine at Christmas but stolid serried ranks of them, growing upwards and downwards acre upon acre, mile after mile, are an enervating eyesore.

The Forestry Commission in Scotland during the last generation has had a bewildering obsession with altering the landscape of the country by planting these awful trees into every conceivable inch of ground as if it, in a recurring nightmare, were plunging the St Andrew's Cross into the summit of Everest.

Over 90 per cent of the afforested area of Scotland is crammed with Sitka spruce, Japanese larch or lodgepole pine. And the cost of newsprint and paper continues to rise.

CRICHTON CASTLE

The rugged ruins of Crichton Castle stand on the right bank of the River Tyne not far from Gorebridge, though Crichton Castle is not to be confused with Borthwick Castle, also near Gorebridge. It is awesome and menacing, a chunky fortress now in the care of Historic Scotland.

The keep on the east side was built in the fourteenth century by John de Crichton. His son, also John, was twice Chancellor of Scotland, first from 1439–44 and then from 1448–53. His enemies, the Douglases, besieged and despoiled Crichton in 1444, when the Chancellor was conveniently out of the way in Edinburgh. Undeterred, he rebuilt and extended the castle. His grandson was taken hostage in 1483 for plotting against James III, and as a result the castle was forfeit. Thereafter it changed hands a number of times before being claimed in 1581 by Francis Stewart, 5th Earl of Bothwell, son of John Stewart, illegitimate son of James V and Jean, sister of James Hepburn, 4th Earl of Bothwell, if you can work that one out.

Inside the medieval walls, Francis Stewart created a Renaissance palace with corbels, panelled ceilings, lavish rooms with grand fireplaces, and a carved Renaissance staircase. He also devised the courtyard with its seven-bay arcade and diamond-faceted stonework. In 1595 Stewart fled abroad in disgrace, and James VI ordered Crichton Castle to be razed. Instead, the castle was allowed to fade away.

Its carcass was memorialized by Sir Walter Scott in his long narrative poem 'Marmion' in 1808:

*Crichton! Though now
  thy miry court
But pens the lazy steer and sheep
Thy turrets rude, and totter'd
  keep;
Have been the minstrel's loved
  abode
Oft have I traced within thy fort,
Of mould'ring shields the mystic
  sense,
Scutcheons of honour, or pretence,
Quarter'd in old armorial sort
Remains of rude magnificence.*

21

22

DRYBURGH ABBEY

The Borders are rich with abbeys. Founded in the twelfth century, that at Melrose is the most majestic; that at Jedburgh the most complete; that at Kelso a twelfth-century 'stump'. Dryburgh Abbey, only a frame or shell left to echo its turbulent history, sits (or stands) by the banks of the River Tweed. The ruins are nicely framed by trees and lush greenery.

The two homosexual English kings, Richard II and Edward II, torched Dryburgh in 1322 and 1385, respectively, the building finally being destroyed in 1544. In 1700 the land and the ruins of the Abbey were acquired by one Thomas Haliburton, Sir Walter Scott's great-grandfather.

Scott, although born in Edinburgh (1771–1832), was very much a Borders man. From 1812 he lived in his great pile of a folly, Abbotsford, near Melrose. One of the major and most influential writers of his time, his best novels include *The Heart of Midlothian*, *Redgauntlet*, *Old Mortality* and *Rob Roy*. The latter has been much read recently, as a result of the release of a popular film of the same title which has little to do with Scott's novel.

Walter Scott's bones are laid out at Dryburgh, as is the body of Field-Marshal Earl Haig, victor at Mons, Ypres and the Somme during the First World War with outrageous human cost. Dryburgh Abbey's tranquillity totally contrasts with this image.

DUNS CASTLE

Duns Castle, albeit incorporating part of the 'original' tower built around 1320, may look the real McCoy but it's a Gothic (or Gothick) re-creation, pretty enough none the less and that's how we like our ruined castles these Heritage days. Needless to say, the beastly English destroyed the castle in the sixteenth century. After all, what else were the English and history for? Castles too?

The blue in the centre of the photograph to the right is not of some mighty Borders river but an artificial loch, which lends romance to the setting. The castle occupies a pleasing seat a mile from Duns, until 1975 the neat and tidy county town of Berwickshire. Duns may or may not (legend again) have been the birthplace of medieval philosopher Duns Scotus; it was the birthplace of racing driver, Jim Clark.

The loch and wildlife area around the castle are managed by the National Trust for Scotland, a power for the good throughout the country and most emphatically not a 'branch' or subsidiary of the English National Trust.

23

FARMING IN THE BORDERS

A field is a field is a field. Not to a farmer it isn't.

When I grew up in Edinburgh in the 1940s and 1950s we were taught to revere farmers and farming. It was thanks to their work, their vocation, that those of us in the cities were able to prosper. And when we went to visit our cousins in Kelso in Roxburghshire we were quietly impressed to see farmers at work.

By then, of course, horses were on the way out. Ploughs were pulled by tractors, and the blades of combine harvesters glistened in the occasional sun. The fields *smelled* of life enhancement, sustenance.

Ayrshire still has its dairy cattle. Thanks to its high rainfall from the prevailing south-westerly winds, its pasture tends to be brilliant green, providing much pleasure to munching cows.

The other picture shows the patterns made by a plough in a field just north of Berwick-upon-Tweed. There is such dignity in a ploughed field, the furrows left behind, waiting for the yearly cycle to begin again.

ROAD JUST NORTH OF BERWICK-UPON-TWEED

Sir Walter Scott, the Laird of Abbotsford in the Borders, was very much aware that Berwick-upon-Tweed was in English hands:

*March, march, Ettrick
   and Teviotdale,
Why the deil dinna ya march
   forward in order?
March, march, Eskdale
   and Liddesdale,
All the Blue Bonnets are bound
   for the Border.*

The Monastery (1820)

Strathclyde

HOLY ISLAND

The two-mile-long hump of Holy Island is well named, although until 1830 it was called Lamlash, now the name of the town on the island of Arran which it faces a mile away, with Lamlash Bay in between. Before then it was called St Molaise or St Mo Las after the Columban monk who, in the sixth century, withdrew from the world and shored up in a cave at the base of the island's mightiest mountain, Mullach Mor, surviving, our old friend legend has it, until he was 120.

The ruins of a fourteenth-century monastery further attest to the island's sanctity. The lighthouse, at the bottom of the photograph on this page, might also be taken as having religious symbolism. Goats climb the crags and now share the place with monks from the Samye Ling Buddhist monastery at Eskdalemuir in Dumfriesshire who purchased the island in 1992 for use as a retreat for meditation.

30

ISLE OF ARRAN

The island of Arran – twenty miles long, ten miles wide – lodges in the Firth of Clyde, fourteen miles from the mainland to the east and four miles from the Kintyre peninsula to the west. It is a favourite Scottish holiday resort and innumerable people in Glasgow and Edinburgh have weekend and holiday homes there. The population is 3,500 but during the summer months rises to three times that.

The northern half of the island is mountainous, the highest peak being Goat Fell (2,868 feet, falling short of being a Munro by 132 feet). Beinn Bhreac (2,332 feet) and Beinn Tarsuinn (2,706 feet) may be observed from many viewpoints in west Scotland, and

enhance the prospect from the mainland. They can even be seen on a fine day from high-rise buildings in Glasgow. The southern part of Arran is geographically less exciting, a gentler terrain. Because of the great variety of the island's landscape, geologists are passionate about the place.

Arran has 56 miles of coast road but only two roads cross the island. The main town is Brodick, which is also the principal ferry port. The town has a population of about 1,000, and lots of little hotels, guest houses and shops snuggle together. Brodick Castle, previously a home of the Dukes of Hamilton, is now owned by the National Trust for Scotland.

The island has a long and lively

history, like most parts of Scotland. There are Neolithic cairns dotted about, and standing stones and stone circles from the Bronze Age. Arran was sacked by the Vikings in 797, and didn't become part of the Kingdom of Scotland until 1266 and the Treaty of Perth. During the grim Cromwellian interlude the island was occupied. Even more grimly, during the nineteenth century major Clearances of people were undertaken to foist large-scale, enclosed sheep farms on Arran. One-third of the population emigrated which, as John and Julia Keay's *Collins Encyclopaedia of Scotland* puts it, 'effectively killed off Gaelic culture on the island'.

CULZEAN CASTLE

Infinitely more palace than fort, Culzean Castle perches above the bay from which it takes its name, near Maybole, overlooking the Clyde with the rugged Atlantic beyond. Commissioned by the Earl of Cassillis, descendant of a Kennedy who married well in 1509, it was built by Scotland's greatest architect, Robert Adam, in association with his brother James, between 1777 and 1790. The strategically useful shelf of land on which the castle was built had been possessed by Kennedy strongholds since the twelfth century – first another castle, then a fortified house.

As well as being Robert Adam's masterpiece in Scotland, Culzean is the most magnificent of all the country's grand homes, devised to endorse the Kennedys of Carrick as the most powerful family in south-west Scotland. Adam's creation marries a Gothic exterior, complete with crenellations and a drum tower on the sea side, as well as courtyard and clock tower, to a Georgian interior with elegant oval staircase. The landscaped park was designed by Alexander Nasmyth and occupies 565 acres. It features exotic shrubs and trees as well as a Gothic camellia house, a pond and aviary.

31

GLASGOW

Glasgow may be irritated by not being Scotland's capital city but for two centuries it was known to everyone as 'the second city of the Empire'; and we all know whose the Empire was. With a population now of approximately 600,000, Glasgow is the country's largest city and its thriving commerical centre.

Both romantically and practically, shipbuilding on the River Clyde was the heart of Glasgow; its proud pulse. In the last thirty years almost every shipyard and engineering works has shut down and, until recently, Glasgow's self-confidence was shaken. In the 1980s, the city came to life again, challenging, then overtaking Edinburgh in many of the capital's traditional areas of expertise. The superb gallery on the Pollock Estate designed by Barry Gasson to house the Burrell Collection was opened in 1983. In 1988 the Glasgow Garden Festival was a triumph, and in 1990 Glasgow was chosen as European City of Culture. In 1996 it is Europe's City of Architecture. It has three universities, and Scotland's new Roman Catholic cardinal, Thomas Winning, lives there.

The neo-Gothic building with its mass of arches in the centre of the picture is Glasgow University, designed by Sir Gilbert Scott in 1870 and only vaguely resembles another of his great designs: St Pancras railway station. The buildings towards the bottom left of the photograph are Glasgow Art Gallery and Museum in Kelvingrove Park. The art gallery houses what is probably the most distinguished civic collection in the UK. The Scottish Colourists are finely represented, although the best-known, or most notorious, picture in the gallery is Salvador Dali's slick and shiny *Christ of St John on the Cross*. University and art gallery are bisected by the River Kelvin. In the distance are the Campsie Fells, Glasgow's very own hills.

GLASGOW

At first glance, Park Circus – in the centre of the picture – could be Bath or Brighton. It is, however, Kelvingrove Park, surrounded by foliage. In the last century it was a much-sought-after residential area; Glasgow's most successful attempt at Victorian town planning and architecture.

Immediately above this confident architecture and lush greenery is an area called Woodlands, known in the 1980s as Glasgow's Square Mile of Murder owing to a particularly gruesome death.

North of it is the Great Western Road and the quaintly named Cowcaddens, originally common grazing ground for cattle, where the Theatre Royal (home of Scottish National Opera) is located, and where Scottish Television has its studios. Buchanan Street bus station is nearby.

33

GLASGOW

The best cities are built around rivers, and Glasgow on the River Clyde is no exception. Tradition has it (tradition always does) that a saint came here, or rather two: first St Ninian, Scotland's earliest-known Christian leader, around AD 400, then Kentigern, or Mungo, some time in the sixth century. The city's coat of arms incorporates objects associated, according to legend, with St Mungo's miracles: a bird, a tree, a fish, a ring and a bell.

In the foreground is the railway viaduct across the river, leading into Central Station. The Edwardian building exudes tremendous style and confidence, and has thirteen platforms. It gleams and shines. The lowest bridge in the photograph is George V Bridge, the memorial stone of which was laid by that monarch in 1927. The bridge above the railway viaduct is Glasgow Bridge, commonly known as Jamaica Bridge, the major north–south route during Glasgow's nineteenth-century nirvana. Which leaves the elegant and slender suspension bridge, approximately 100 years old and for the use of pedestrians only.

To the right, near the centre of the picture is the glass and steel of St Enoch's Centre, a fairly hideous – 'controversial' and 'arresting' are more generous adjectives – shopping 'centre', opened in 1989. Presumably some people patronize it more than once as otherwise it would go out of business. Looking up and into the photograph, are the inevitable, ubiquitous high-rise blocks and a view towards Glasgow's second university, Strathclyde.

GLASGOW

Glaswegians have always relished a good fair. Way back in 1190 King William I ('The Lion', whose heraldic device of a lion rampant was eventually adopted as Scotland's quarter of the Royal Standard, and the Lion, or Lyon, became Scotland's King of Arms) granted Glasgow the right to hold an annual fair. During the nineteenth century this fair (held at the octave of St Peter and St Paul, from 7 July) was made to coincide with the Glasgow trade holiday week.

In the nineteenth century the fair started to be held on Glasgow Green, where this photograph was taken. Clearly it consists of nothing more special than the usual rides, stalls and attractions of funfairs anywhere today.

In 1990 Glasgow Council set about reviving more traditional fair entertainment including juggling and dancing, singing and theatrical events on a site near the People's Palace gallery and museum.

36

GLASGOW

Glasgow's post-Second World War
architecture is mostly a disgrace.
In a frenzy of social conscience
(or something purporting to that),
Glasgow's city fathers set about
demolishing the city's Victorian
tenements – most famously those in the
Gorbals in the 1970s – and rehoused
the 'officially incompetent' in grim
high-rise tower blocks, often praised
at the time by earnest architectural
critics. The flats in this photograph
are in Dalmarnoch in the East End,
specifically the Miller and Ardenlea
Streets flats.

Architects of the reputation of Sir
Basil Spence, who designed many of

Glasgow's most benumbing blocks,
wouldn't, of course, have deigned to
live in such prisons themselves. The
city is now pockmarked with less than
dear green places where some of the
most unappetizing high-rise building
has, literally, been exploded and,
chunk of concrete by chunk of
concrete, blown out of existence.
Tragically, while watching one of
Spence's buildings in its death throes
in 1994, an elderly woman was killed;
a horrible epitaph to something that
should never have been.

It is tempting to speculate that
Spence's buildings were an unsubtle
snook cocked at Glasgow by an
architect educated in Edinburgh.

GLASGOW

Roofs in East Glasgow these may be,
but of more significance are the three
words stolidly emblazoned upon them:
'MORTON', 'CELTIC' and 'RANGERS'. It
is debatable whether golf or football is
more Scotland's national game – today
more people play golf than watch
football – but 'fitba' (not to be
confused with rugby, or rugger) is a
national obsession; almost a religion.

Rangers and Celtic, jointly known
as 'The Old Firm', are Glasgow's
leading teams, and here are their
colours on the roofs. Rangers, who
play at Ibrox, came into being in 1873;
Celtic whose ground is Parkhead, in
1888. From its earliest years Celtic
was predominantly, but not exclusively,
composed of players of Irish extraction
and was thus, predominantly but not
exclusively, Roman Catholic. By way
of contrast, Rangers picked up the kilt
of Protestantism. There was a bit of a
shindy in 1989 when Rangers signed
Mo Johnston, the first known Catholic
to play for the hitherto Protestant
team.

Similarly in Edinburgh, Heart of
Midlothian, colloquially known as
Hearts, is regarded as the Protestant
team; Hibernian, or Hibs, as the
Catholic, although the Catholic
population in Edinburgh is minuscule
compared with that of Glasgow.

'Morton' is the name of the Clyde
town of Greenock's football team
(founded in 1874), its ground at
Cappielow.

37

GLASGOW

I don't think this is a bus depot but Jason Hawkes, our brilliant photographer, does. If it is a bus depot it's hard to see how any of the buses other than those in the outer two rows could make their escape; although it has to be conceded that the colour of the bus tops suggest they wear the livery of one company.

The picture defeats me as to where it is and, more significantly, defeats my Glasgow relatives and friends, but I'd guess that it is a sports ground, with spectators having been bussed in from Strathclyde. Maybe they are sitting in the grey-roofed grandstand watching some thrilling activity on the pitch or court to the right of the picture, but it all looks suspiciously silent to me.

GLASGOW

When you drive through or about Glasgow you have some idea of the city's size. It's a big place. In this photograph, across the Clyde in the centre, is the expressway to Broomhill, where as it happens my sister-in-law and her family live. Her husband, an electrician, has spent time on the oil rigs; she worked as a systems analyst in the Govan shipyard – in the foreground of the picture, on this side of the Clyde – of Kvaerner, a Norwegian company which took it over from the previous owners when it was on the verge of bankruptcy. HMS *Ocean*, the ship that sank the famous Swan Hunter yard, was launched by Kvaerner Govan in October 1995. The 20,500-tonne ship is the first purpose-built helicopter-landing ship built for the Royal Navy, and the first warship built at the Govan yard since 1970.

My brother-in-law is an islander, brought up in the faith of the Free Church of Scotland; my sister-in-law is a Roman Catholic. Glasgow is that sort of city, and it is to be hoped there is more tolerance in it today than there has been historically.

GOUROCK

Whoever named places on the south bank of the River Clyde clearly had a penchant for the letter G: Giffnock, Port Glasgow, Greenock and Gourock nowadays form a continuous ribbon of development. Gourock, unlike its neighbours, is rather a jolly place, with marines and a bustling pier from which sea-smelling ferries set sail to Dunoon and other northern ports.

The town has long had a reputation for sea bathing. In these somewhat genteel times, with everyone fussing about the polluted ocean, health-obsessed folk tend to be happier splashing and lazing in a chlorinated swimming pool.

39

Lothian

North of the Borders, east of
Strathclyde, is Lothian, host to glorious
and historic Edinburgh, the country's
capital, with its annual International
Festival of the Arts. There are the Forth
Bridges, the old royal borough of

EDINBURGH CASTLE

Edinburgh Castle, perched on its one-time volcanic rock, is a proud fortification of considerable assurance and pride to the citizens of the Scottish capital, and a marvel to visitors, especially if the sun is shining. These days, it's unlikely to be employed for military purposes, or to defend the capital, but it is the crown which adorns one of the world's most beautiful cities; and the army is still very much in command there.

There has been a fortification on that rock (for many years partly surrounded by an artificially created lake, the Nor' Loch) since the seventh century, and its history has to a considerable degree been almost synonymous with that of Scotland. Today's complex of buildings houses the Honours of Scotland: the monarch's regalia, comprising her crown, sword and sceptre. Queen Margaret's chapel, built in the eleventh century, is the oldest and most exquisite example of Romanesque architecture in the country. There are terrific military museums, and a sternly designed war memorial gravely commemorates the twentieth-century dead. Mons Meg, Scotland's largest cannon, is a menacing sight to behold, even though these days it has been removed from the Castle's ramparts and placed inside a room to preserve it from further metal erosion; and the one o'clock gun, so named because it is fired every day except Sunday from the Castle ramparts to ensure that no one in the Presbyterian city is late for an appointment, is fun.

During the Edinburgh International Festival of the Arts each year in August, the world-renowned military tattoo is held on the Castle esplanade.

The Castle is at the top of the High Street of the Old Town, with Holyrood Palace, the monarch's official residence in Scotland, at the foot. This street is familiarly known as the Royal Mile.

EDINBURGH

At first glance (so often aerial photographs are deceptive) this picture might suggest Edinburgh's New Town. It is, in fact, of the Old Town, showing the High Street – the Royal Mile – just below where the Mound swings round and crosses into George IV Bridge. This is another thoroughfare named after an English, sorry, British monarch, George IV, whose triumphant visit in 1822 was, in a manner of writing, masterminded by Sir Walter Scott.

The crown of St Giles Cathedral, after which I was named – honestly; my father, Esmé Gordon, RSA, FRIBA, was at the time of my birth and for many years thereafter architect to the fabric – is in the centre, to the left. St Giles isn't in fact a cathedral. It is the High Kirk of Edinburgh; 'kirk' being the Scots word for 'church'. In the Church of Scotland all churches or kirks are equal, in the eyes of God if not in the eyes of man.

St Giles' principal time in history was in the 1560s when the last Roman Catholic Mass – most Church of Scotland churches were Catholic buildings – was sung there and Master John Knox (1513–72), the austere and often tedious principal personage of the Scottish Reformation, became minister. When Mary Stewart, only surviving child of Mary of Guise and King James V, became monarch in 1561, St Giles became the tiring house or tilt-yard of the establishment of Presbyterianism. It was there that, on Sunday, 23 July 1637, upon the attempted introduction of the English prayer book, that kailwife Jenny Geddes from the Tron flung her folding-stool at the Dean, and shouted abuse at him.

The arcaded French-influenced building in the centre of the picture is the City Chambers, built as the Royal Exchange by John Adam in 1753–61.

There, the Lord Provost and town council meet and strive to run the city's affairs.

In front of the City Chambers and to the right of the High Kirk is the Mercat (or market) Cross. Today, its main purpose is to allow the magnificently tabarded Lord Lyon King of Arms, the principal Scottish herald, to proclaim the accession of a new monarch. Historically, the Mercat Cross was a place both of entertainment and of execution, and there Deacon Brodie, my favourite Scottish character – town councillor and cabinet maker by day, leader of a gang of crooks by night; subject of a play by Robert Louis Stevenson and W. E. Henley, and inspiration for Dr Jekyll and Mr Hyde – met his maker at the end of a rope on gallows of his own devising.

Behind the City Chambers are the roofs of Waverley railway station, whose trains today bring more Scots back to Edinburgh than take them away from it. As Dr Johnson didn't say, 'When a Scotsman's tired of London, it's about time he came back to Edinburgh.'

EDINBURGH

The grime-encrusted edifice to the right and centre of the picture is not a Victorian attempt at a Jules Verne rocketship but a misguided memorial to Scotland's greatest novelist, Sir Walter Scott, inevitably known as the Scott Monument.

It was designed by a joiner, George Meikle Kemp, who entered a public competition to design a suitable memorial for the Laird of Abbotsford. As is the way with architectural competitions, Kemp's design originally came third, but his concept was 'developed' and his vision was selected, then built between 1840 and 1846. There is a narrow, obscure staircase within it and many suicides have plunged to Princes Street Gardens from high up, silently observed by a Carrara marble statue of Sir Walter, sitting underneath the black arches at the base, accompanied, in a Landseer-like way, by his faithful deerhound, Maida.

Dotted about the Monument are statues depicting characters from Scott's novels. Recently the city, or the District (it is both difficult and unrewarding to try to keep up with local politics), resolved to clean the blackened soot-engrained stump, but had it proceeded the Monument might have disintegrated, so delicate apparently is the sandstone. A merciful release, I'd have said, as the neo-Gothic steeple is an eyesore upon Princes Street Gardens.

Mind you, as one of the most famous streets in the world, Princes Street in recent decades has descended to nothing more than yet another indifferent shopping mall, albeit one with a spectacular view of Princes Street Gardens and the Castle across the road.

45

EDINBURGH

The Tron Kirk, tucked into the High Street where it meets the Bridges, the street running from the east end of Princes Street towards the university, is the time-honoured tryst of Hogmanay revellers. Like so many Church of Scotland buildings these days, the doors were until recently locked, even on Sunday (the deconsecrated church is now a tourists' information centre). The building, designed to give refuge to the congregation from St Giles when it was (whisper it not) raised to an ecclesiastical cathedral, suffered an unusual indignity in 1824 when the steeple plunged into the street during the terrifying fire which devastated the south side of the High Street from the Tron up to St Giles.

These days, fewer people are sick on the steps of the Tron on New Year's morning than was the case a generation ago. Maybe they're all sick in their homes.

EDINBURGH

Murrayfield, in west Edinburgh,
is the national stadium which seats (we
used to stand, when young, and paid
less for the privilege) 55,000 spectators
or fans and where Rugby Union
'internationals' are played against
Foreign Countries, including England,
Ireland, Wales and France, and visiting
countries such as New Zealand (the
Springboks) and South Africa (the
All Blacks, who are, bewilderingly,
still all white). 'SRU' are the initials of
the Scottish Rugby Union, and Rugby
Union (as opposed to Rugby League)
was, until decreed otherwise in August
1995, an entirely amateur game.

The Scotland versus England
annual game, played alternately at
Twickenham in Middlesex and at
Murrayfield, is the apex of the Scottish
Rugby Union year. Since 1879, the
match has been played for the Calcutta
Cup, which is a bit like competing
for the Stone of Scone under the
coronation chair in Westminster
Abbey.

Like all sports, and increasingly as
sport tries to take itself more seriously,
rugby is crammed with innumerable
fixtures and features. On the
international level, this includes the
Grand Slam (one country beating the
other four), the Triple Crown (one
home country beating the other three)
and the Five Nations Championship.

There is a serious amount of club
rugby in Scotland, played particularly
by the old boys (not *that* old) of public
– that is, private, and mostly fee-paying
– schools, and of clubs notably in the
Borders, a more modern version
perhaps of cattle rustling. Rugby Union
is very much a game for the middle
classes, and for those aspiring thus.

EDINBURGH

St Peter's, Lutton Place in Newington,
is a Scottish Episcopal Church rather
than Church of Scotland, the country's
established, official church. The
Episcopal Church (its worshippers
colloquially known as 'Piscies') has
been a non-established, independent,
Protestant Scottish Church since
1690. It is a branch of the worldwide
Anglican community. The Church
is disestablished and, in spite of
what is often assumed, independent
of, but in communion with, the
Church of England.

EDINBURGH

Edinburgh is my home. I was born here, educated here and, after more than thirty years in London, have recently returned to live in one of the prettiest streets in the Georgian New Town. The New Town, largest city development in the world, was begun in 1767 and completed around 1830. It covers an area of about one square mile and contains more than 10,000 listed buildings, most of them still private residences. Inside and out, the houses are beautifully preserved and looked after. Edinburgh, today, is a rich city, though it's often hard to tell where the private money comes from.

The Old Town, around the Royal Mile with the Castle at the top, Holyrood Palace at the bottom, is to the south side of the Mound and Princes Street, the New Town to the north, and it is built downhill from the apex of magisterial George Street (forgetting Princes Street, long since ruined by town planners). On a fine day the Firth of Forth and the 'wee kingdom' of Fife may be easily and enjoyably observed from George Street, sometimes giving the impression, because of the gradient and perspective, that the sea will embrace and envelop Scotland's capital.

The New Town – its creation employed the genius of such architects as James Craig, Robert Adam and William Playfair – consists of a dozen or more developments of streets, squares and circuses, all laid out in classical symmetry. The houses were built of sandstone from Craigleith quarry. On a wet day, and there are plenty of those, the New Town can look uniformly grey, austere and unyielding, disinclined to yield its secrets. On sparkling days, the stone of the façades seems to be lined with a rainbow of subtle colours, ranging from pinkish grey through yellowish brown and greyish orange to dusky brown. Overall, the effect is usually of

silvery grey. Charlotte Square and St Andrew Square, one at each end of George Street, are particularly elegant; the Georgian House in Charlotte Square, administered by the National Trust for Scotland, shows what town houses in Edinburgh would have been like when first built and inhabited.

The New Town contributes magnificently to making Edinburgh quite one of the most beautiful cities in Europe, even in the world.

The bridge took seven years to build in the 1880s, and in the process cost the lives of 57 men. Among mind-numbing statistics, it incorporates 55,000 tons of steel and eight million rivets, the eight-millionth one being piled into position in 1890 by that well-known riveter, Edward VIII, then Prince of Wales.

For many years it has been said that the Forth Bridge is constantly being painted, except possibly on Hogmanay, with a particular red paint to combat rust to the steel. In recent years, owing to the costs involved, painting has been less constant.

The *Scotsman* reported on 24 August 1995 that 'Painting work on the Forth Bridge will more than double next year and will be done by a private company. Railtrack's decision that 6,000 metres of the bridge are to be painted in 1995–96 was welcomed by campaigners who had complained about the rusty appearance of the steelwork. A Railtrack spokeswoman denied that protests about the bridge's condition had led to the increase in painting. "You do not manage a bridge on whims", she said, before conceding: "Nobody likes criticism. If you can do something to make people happy, you do. The bridge is going to look better than it has for the last five years."' The painting contract has been awarded to an Aberdeen firm with wide experience of working on oil rigs.

The other bridge, to be seen in the foreground of the photograph, is the coolly modern Forth Road Bridge. Opened in 1964, it resulted in the demise of the cumbersome car ferries which used to ply the Firth from South Queensferry to North Queensferry. It remains a toll bridge, so remember to have small change handy whenever you need to cross it. It's a perfect complement and counterpart to the Rail Bridge though drivers have to be careful of biting winds as they steer their cars across.

THE FORTH BRIDGES

After more than fifty years I still experience a thrill every time I see that nineteenth-century engineering Wonder of the World, the Forth Rail Bridge, which umbilically takes possession of the kingdom nine miles west of Edinburgh at South Queensferry. It connects, crucially, the south of Scotland to what comes above it. When you stand admiring it, you hear and see trains to Dundee and Aberdeen and elsewhere north thunder and rumble over it. Looking up and across the Firth of Forth, the cantilevered bridge is awesome.

During the Second World War the Luftwaffe tried repeatedly to bomb and destroy the rail bridge, but its thin mass of metal girders was, like a hole-in-one in golf, a virtually impossible target to aim for from an aircraft. Its destruction would have caused national chaos.

THE BASS ROCK

Like the Forth Bridge, the Bass Rock –
in the Firth of Forth three miles north-
east of North Berwick and best viewed,
with binoculars, from Tantallon Castle
– is one of the great land (or sea)
marks near Edinburgh; a giant's
discarded tooth or sugarlump. It was
originally volcanic. Today it houses
buildings including a lighthouse (which
could do with a spot of whitewash)
and the ruins of a sixteenth-century
chapel. It's a bird sanctuary on
which dwells a colony of gannets
and silly, endearing puffins. Earnest
ornithologists, armed with anoraks,
Barbours and binoculars, are its main
visitors these days, braving the fishy
stench. The less obsessive can, seas
permitting, sail around the island
on cruises from North Berwick.
In the seventeenth century, the Rock
took possession of prisoners, first
Covenanters, then Jacobites, showing
the pragmatism of the Scots character.

50

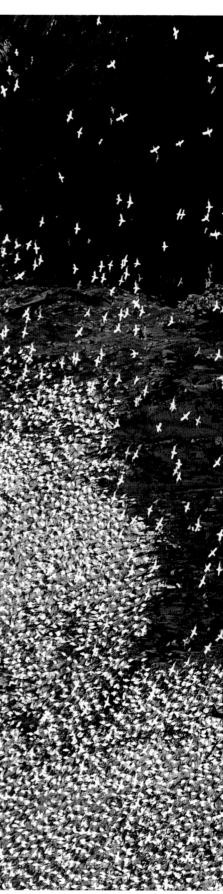

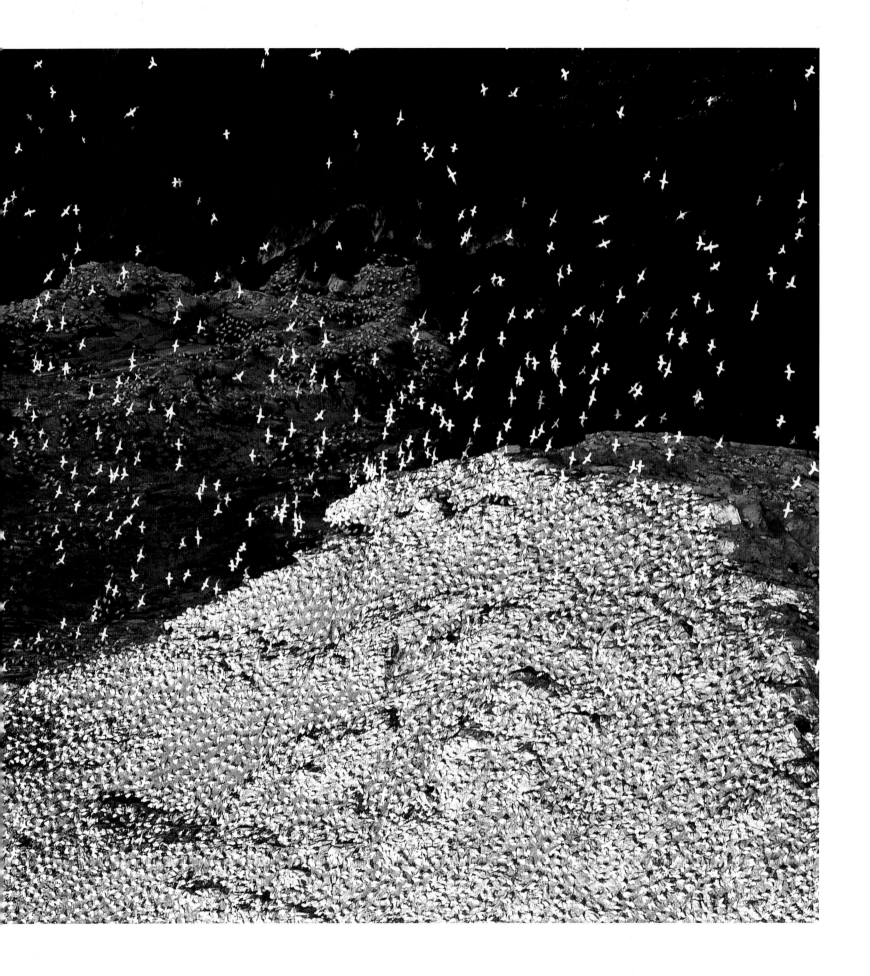

BIRDS IN LOTHIAN

These birds were photographed in Lothian but they could be anywhere, in that a strain of the Scottish character – more Dedalus than Icarus – is passionate about birds, and not only the killing and eating of them. There are eighty bird reserves throughout the country, mostly managed by the Royal Society for the Protection of Birds and the Nature Conservancy Council.

The most romantic sea-bird colony is at St Kilda in the Outer Hebrides. It is also the most isolated. There, over one million sea birds breed each summer. Loch Garten in Speyside has been world famous since 1954 when ospreys, birds of prey that feed on fish, returned to breed. Their annual progress, or otherwise, occupies countless column inches and photographs annually in the national and international press.

FARMING IN LOTHIAN

East Lothian, ripe with barley, is sometimes known as the granary of Scotland, although these golden fields are also common in Fife and Morayshire. All three areas share low rainfall and high sunshine statistics.

Here, as on page 24, a solitary farmer ploughs his field. It is hard to meet a farmer these days who isn't bitter or at least cynical about what the European Community agricultural policies have done to his life. Farmers are paid not to produce food. Fat cheques go into their pockets for neglecting land (set-aside schemes) rather than farming it. Such enforced idleness is alien to the Presbyterian work ethic.

Central

DUNSTAFFNAGE CASTLE

Dunstaffnage Castle, four miles east of Oban, is merely the shell of a keep dating from the thirteenth century. It is chunkily Norman, more Romanesque than picturesque but important none the less. 'Dun' means hill or hill-fort, and Dunstaffnage Castle is perched on the promontory of the River Staff.

This oddly isolated place has experienced its share of history. Robert the Bruce, when Robert I, captured the castle in 1309. Embarrassingly, if you're still haunted by the massacre of Glencoe, he handed over the constabulary to a Campbell; and in 1409 the chief Campbell of that day and henceforth, the (1st) Earl of Argyll, was granted tenure in perpetuity. In both 1554 and 1625 the Campbells bashed the MacDonalds (maybe they were attempting to stamp out, in the land of haggis, incipient hamburgers), and in 1654 they had a go at the nice MacLeans from Mull.

Flora MacDonald, Bonnie Prince Charlie's friend, was imprisoned in Dunstaffnage before she was consigned to the Tower of London. She was released in time for Dr Johnson and Mr Boswell to meet her in Skye in 1773.

Glensanda Quarry

What a devastation of the land is here. Glensanda Quarry, Morvern, is today the largest quarry in Scotland. Seven million tonnes of crushed granite are extracted annually and exported. The nineteenth century was the peak of extraction from the Scottish earth's surface. Coal, iron, slate, sandstone and granite quarrying might have continued to a greater extent than it does (market forces prevailing) had oil and gas not been significantly discovered in the sea surrounding Scotland.

The Scots used to like granite for building. Aberdeen, which sparkles in the sunlight, is still known as the granite city, and Peterhead was substantially built with the rock. London liked red granite in the last century – the Albert Hall is built from granite extracted from the quarries on the Ross of Mull.

For the future, the environment rather than the economy will dictate the use of quarries. They are an eyesore, suggesting the world of blasted planets and science fiction rather than of a civilized, sophisticated twentieth-century society.

OBAN

Oban, the main town of the west Highlands, is one of those places which has its being because if it didn't exist, somewhere else similar would have to. It's a cramped little town, dourly Victorian, in an important geographical spot, where everything appears overpriced. The traffic is a nightmare. Restaurants, cafés and hotels seem exhausted by life and are, to put it politely, uninspiring.

Although people do go on holiday there, Oban's principal function is as the main port to the Hebrides. Before the automobile, it saw more elegant days, with bands tootling on the Corran Esplanade, and MacBrayne's famous ferries preparing to sail to Mull, Inverness, Iona, Staffa, Skye, Barra, South Uist, Colonsay and Oronsay and other exotic locations.

The poet, novelist and short-story writer Iain Crichton Smith lived in Oban, where for many years he taught at the High School. Up-and-coming novelist Alan Warner was brought up there, where he worked on the railways.

Oban's only architectural interest is MacCaig's Folly, which commands the town from above. An unfinished and rather ridiculous would-be replica of the Colosseum in Rome, its creation was funded in the 1890s by a worthy local banker desirous of creating work for the district.

59

INVERARAY

It is tempting to speculate that Inveraray, a pretty little place and one-time county town of Argyll, is the creation of Dr Johnson and James Boswell, who visited it in 1773, then published, respectively, their still readable and fascinatingly relevant *A Journey to the Western Islands of Scotland* (1775) and *Journal of a Tour to the Hebrides* (1785).

Today, Inveraray is architecturally the most handsome town in the Highlands, designed by William Adam and Roger Morris, with the work itself carried out by William's elder son, John, and Robert Mylne, starting in 1744. Dr Johnson had his first experience of whisky at Inveraray Inn, apparently remarking beforehand, 'Come, let me know what it is that makes a Scotchman happy!'

Inveraray is in the heart of Campbell country, and its castle is the seat of the Duke of Argyll, leader of the clan. If you think there are an awful lot of Campbells in the world, perhaps this should be blamed on the 6th Duke, who died in 1839 without legitimate issue but who is said to have fathered 398 children outside wedlock.

The present castle is eighteenth-century, largely the creation of the town's four architects. Campbells flock to the castle which remains the home of the present Duke of Argyll. Within the Victorian neo-Gothic walls are one of the finest eighteenth-century classical interiors in the UK.

Neil Munro (1864–1930), who wrote the *Para Handy* tales, was born in Inveraray.

62

STIRLING

Stirling, both the castle and the town, are probably more associated with the thirteenth- and fourteenth-century Wars of Independence than any other single place, with the exception of Bannockburn, two miles south. In 1297, seventeen years before the Battle of Bannockburn, Sir William Wallace – Scotland's greatest patriot and the hero of Stirling – routed the Earl of Surrey's English army at the Battle of Stirling Bridge. Wallace marched south and captured Berwick-upon-Tweed, an event which was always a fillip to Scots pride. In 1298, he was made guardian of the realm.

Later that year, Edward I, 'The Hammer of the Scots', marched north with his troops, to revenge Surrey's defeat, and at the closely fought Battle of Falkirk the English longbows finally defeated the meagre Scottish cavalry, under Sir John Comyn. Wallace went under cover to reorganize but in 1305 was betrayed to the English by Sir John de Menteith, an envious fellow Scot who had bowed the knee to Edward in return for trivial favours.

It wasn't until the 1860s that the Wallace Monument, with its distinctive, almost sculptural, Gothic crown, was built on Abbey Craig, where it dominates Stirling and the surrounding countryside. The tower may be climbed and the view from the top on a clear day is quite something.

For centuries, Stirling's geographic position made the importance of the castle and town fundamental to the well-being of the country. The place acted as a bridge between the Highlands and Lowlands as nowhere else did, being between Edinburgh and Glasgow and north of both. Although Stirling was frequently the centre of government, it was never the country's capital. For centuries it was an important commercial centre.

The castle, built high up on a crag of basaltic rock, quite closely resembles Edinburgh Castle. In 1304, Edward I besieged the fortress for twelve weeks, employing catapults and mangonels. Lead for the catapults' counterweights was looted from the roofs of churches

in the area. The English laid claim to the castle but lost it again after Bannockburn. It was rebuilt in the fifteenth century and in the 1540s became a royal palace. James V built a wing with a Renaissance façade of windows, niches and statues. The castle was essentially so impregnable that it could readily be used as a palace as well. It is now the headquarters of the Argyll and Sutherland Highlanders, whose museum houses it. The view from the ramparts over the Forth, Stirling Bridge and vast acres of Scotland is magnificent.

Stirling is very much a holiday centre these days. It also houses, in Bridge of Allan to its north, Stirling University. Founded in 1967, this is a genuinely new university, not some superannuated Poly or renamed College of Higher Education.

CASTLE CAMPBELL

Castle Campbell, when seen from further back than this photograph, looks as if it might be situated in a Middle East desert. It is set securely on an outcrop of rock between burns named Care and Sorrow, and until the 1st Earl of Argyll acquired it as part of his marriage settlement at the end of the fifteenth century it was understandably known as Castle Gloom. In addition, it resides in the parish of Dollar, Scots for dolour. All very *Pilgrim's Progress*, and therefore appropriate that the biggest Roundhead of them all, Lord Protector Oliver Cromwell and his inaptly named henchman, General Monk, should have burned the castle in 1654.

Colin Campbell, 1st Earl of Argyll, understandably changed the name of the fortress to that of his family name, and Castle Campbell was quickly adopted as the main seat of the Argyll family in the Lowlands. The ruins are handsome, particularly the well-preserved high rectangular tower, and since 1948 the castle has been in state hands.

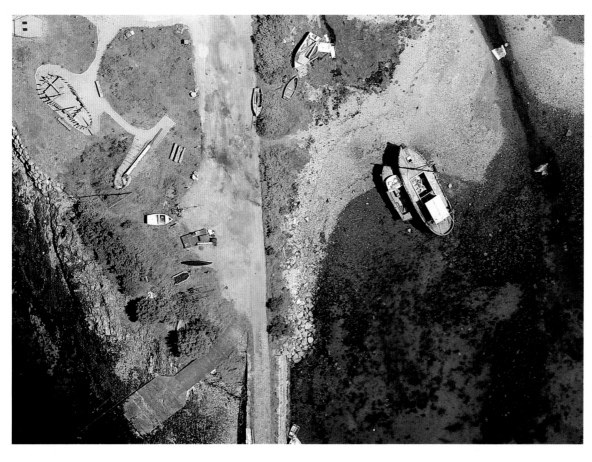

ISLAND OF MULL

The island of Mull, off the coast of Argyll, has a land area of 353 square miles, 120 miles of increasingly reliable roads, and a population of 2,400. In 1821 the population was over 10,000, since when it has declined, although it's probably stabilized now. Many of the islanders today are 'White Settlers'. In his incisive *Romantic Scotland*, Charles Maclean rightly says that Mull 'has become as overgrown with retired colonels and bank managers as Tunbridge Wells'. Indeed, in the proliferation of boutiques and shops catering to tourists you're hard put to hear a Scots accent rather than those of the English minor public schools.

Mull is a picturesque island, and the main 'town' Tobermory is a colourful haven from often foul weather if not from the fiend, with colourful houses nestling around the lively harbour.

Ben More, at 3,170 feet, qualifies as a 'Munro' and commands the centre of Mull. It provides, as do so many high points in the Highlands and Islands, spectacular views. There are ruins of castles, including Duart Castle near Craignure, restored by Colonel Sir Fitzroy MacLean, 26th Chief of the Clan MacLean, in 1911. Within boating distance are the islands of Colonsay, Islay and Jura to the south, and, Coll, Tiree and Iona to the west.

Mull is better served by ferries than many of the islands. The car ferry from Oban to Craignure, which throbs through the waters at high speed, takes 45 minutes.

65

Tayside

Dundee

Dundee – erstwhile industrial city
of the three j's: jute, jam and journalism
– sits on the north shore of the Firth
of Tay, north-west of St Andrews.
The city's early prosperity came from
manufacturing and trading in linen,
although early in the nineteenth century
the industry was hampered by shortages
of flax and later by competition from
Manchester. From 1823 Dundee added
jute to its loom, and by around 1850
the city was known as 'Juteopolis'.
1871 probably marked the apex of
Dundee's prosperity as a textile town,
after which Indian mills, many of them
run by Dundonians, began to undercut
the parent city's prices.

Thereafter Dundee was, frankly,
somewhat run down, as the fat cats
who'd made their fortunes from textiles
invested their cash in North America.
This was so much so that during the
fifties a story was told (apocryphal, of
course) of a delegation of visitors from
the States who were shown around the
city and then entertained by the Lord
Provost at the City Chambers. Everything
they'd seen, they insisted, they did better
in the States. 'What do you think of
Dundee as a whole?' the Lord Provost
eventually asked in some desperation.
'As a hole?' replied the leader of the
American delegation. 'As a hole, we've
never seen anywhere like it.'

Dundee is now a thriving, modern
city, with its population of around
160,000 making a decent living on the
whole. Marmalade is still made there,
and the publishers D. C. Thomson's
Sunday Post remains a Scottish
institution. The *Beano* and *Dandy*,
essential reading in the childhood of all
Scots, continue to flourish.

ARBROATH ABBEY

There are a few key events in every country's history. One of those in Scotland is the Declaration of Arbroath of 1320, popularly called the Declaration of Independence. It was inscribed by eight earls and 31 barons and written not in Lallans but in Latin by the Abbot of Arbroath, Bernard of Linton, Lord Chancellor of Scotland. Pope John XXII had, mischievously and against precedent, declared that Scotland should be subservient to England, and this had encouraged Edward II to march north. He was, as the world knows, routed at Bannockburn in 1314 by Robert the Bruce who thereafter became King Robert I, having freed his nation from English (if not Roman) shackles.

The meagre remains of Arbroath Abbey were, briefly in 1951, the repository for the Stone of Scone or Destiny which had been removed from Westminster Abbey, where it lodged under the coronation chair, by some excitable Scottish nationalists and patriots. The police were not amused, and the sacred chunk of sandstone on which Scottish monarchs had traditionally been crowned was soon returned, presumably not by Scotrail, to Westminster Abbey.

RIVER TAY BRIDGES

As the Firth of Forth has its rail and road bridges, so does the Firth of Tay. The Tay Railway Bridge carries the line from King's Cross, London and Waverley, Edinburgh to Dundee and Aberdeen.

Scotland has many poets but the best-known populist poet has to be Dundee's adopted son – he was born in Edinburgh – William McGonagall (1830–1902). He was akin to a Scottish tabloid laureate, celebrating and reporting events as they occurred. His first book of verse, published in 1877, contained the ever-popular 'Railway Bridge of the Silvery Tay'. A later poem, of 1879, tragically commemorated the disaster of that year, when, during a severe gale, Sir Thomas Bouch's new bridge collapsed and seventy-five passengers (or customers, as they'd be called today) plunged to their deaths with the train into the icy January water. McGonagall's epic includes the mortal lines:

> *So the train mov'd slowly along*
> *the Bridge of Tay.*
> *Until it was midway.*
> *Then the central girders with*
> *a crash gave way.*
> *And down went the train and*
> *passengers into the Tay.*

The stumps of Bouch's bridge, like gravestones, still stick out from the sea as sombre memorial to faulty engineering.

Perhaps mindful of the 1879 disaster, the Tay Road Bridge, officially opened in 1966, clings as low to the water as it reasonably can.

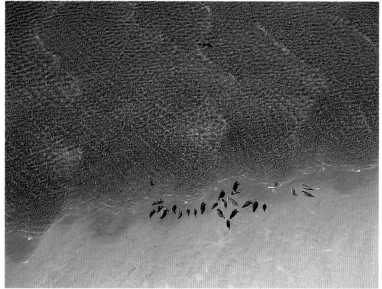

SEALS IN THE FIRTH OF TAY
Not the seal on the Declaration of Arbroath but seals disporting themselves in the Firth of Tay. The Scots are fond of the grey and common seals which bob up around the country's coastline. There are about 75,000 grey seals. In contrast, Scottish waters harbour only about 20,000 common seals, the breed, in spite of its name, being rarer.

As Scotland's smaller islands have become more depopulated, and the peace of the islands and surrounding sea less disturbed, seals have waddled and hobbled out of the water, shaken their sleek pelts, and settled down to the serious business of breeding.

71

KINROSS HOUSE

Not only invading armies from the south but English travellers sometimes visited Scotland in what my young children refer to as the olden days. Daniel Defoe (1660–1731), that vigorous pamphleteer and humane novelist, described Kinross House, Sir William Bruce's Palladian mansion close to Loch Leven, built near the end of the seventeenth century, as 'the most beautiful and regular piece of architecture in all Scotland, perhaps in all Britain'.

The garden is magnificent also; more Italian, as befits the house, than French.

PERTH

Perth is still sometimes known as
'the ancient capital of Scotland', which
once it was; and, more sensibly, as 'the
Fair City'. It has been a royal borough
since the thirteenth century and is the
county town of Perthshire.

It is situated on the west bank of
the Tay, just above the Firth. It is very
much a country town, with agriculture
prominent among its concerns. The
manufacture of linen and cotton were
crucial historically to Perth's well-
being; as was, in a more modest way,
dry-cleaning: Pullar's of Perth is still
a household name throughout the
country.

The city is steeped in history.
John's Knox's sermon in St John's Kirk
on 11 May 1559 was the first blast of
the Reformation. Thereafter, inevitably,
churches and beautiful objects
were desecrated and destroyed, as
if out of fear at what man by way of
beauty was capable of creating. Perth,
partly as a result of this, today lacks
architectural glories.

The Marquis of Montrose
took possession of the city in 1644.
Cromwell (that man again) pilfered
stone from the Greyfriars monastery
to build himself a citadel on the South
Inch, a place also used for jollity and
witch burning. The Jacobites occupied
the city in both 1715 and 1745.

Scone Palace, north-east of Perth,
was the place where Scotland's kings
and queens were enthroned. King
Kenneth MacAlpin (Kenneth I) made
Scone his capital in about 840 and
brought to it the Stone of Scone,
a holy relic from the Middle East,
more romantically known as the
Stone of Destiny. The last coronation
at Scone was that of Charles II in 1651,
centuries after Edward I had purloined
the Stone and deposited it under
the coronation chair in Westminster
Abbey. In spite of the absence of the
Stone, Scone Palace and its grounds
are worth a visit.

73

ANSTRUTHER

This is the most evocative, almost
sensual photograph of the Fife port
of Anstruther, which achieved royal
burgh status in the 1580s. It is still
a favourite summer holiday town
but its winter bites snarling cold. The
breakwaters, like the arms of crabs
embracing the water in the harbour,
do not permit the rude seas beyond
to buffet the gentle haven.

Anstruther used to be Fife's major
fishing port, and earlier than that
sailing ships which traded with the
Baltic were put up here. Sadly, as with
other places on this part of the Fife
coast – Pitenweem, Elie, Crail –
the town is now, to all intents and
purposes, but a former fishing port.

ST ANDREWS

This is, surprisingly, not a golf course, but it is St Andrews on the north-east coast, a unique and precious jewel in the Scottish diadem.

The, to me, inexplicable game of golf – in which grown men and women, frequently muffled up against the weather, endeavour to strike tiny, hard, white balls into 18 almost equally tiny holes hundreds of metres from one another – has been played at St Andrews for nearly 400 years. Would this suggest that there's little else to do at St Andrews? It shouldn't, for in its heyday the town was much involved with education and theology. (When golf was first permitted to be played on a Sunday is another matter.)

The Scots word for 'golf' is 'gowff', and that is how knowing Scots to this day pronounce it. It is unkind to remark that in Scots 'gowff' also means a fool or simpleton.

Most people interested in the obsessive sport pay homage to St Andrews as the begetter of the game, its alma mater. The club here was founded in 1754, later pompously designated 'Royal and Ancient' by King William IV. In 1919 the Royal and Ancient Golf Club, which boasts four courses on which anyone may play upon payment of the appropriate fee, was made responsible for organizing the annual Open competition, the grandest in the game, usually won by bizarrely clad Americans.

Ecclesiastically, St Andrews thrived before the Reformation. The cathedral, begun in 1161 but long reduced to picturesque ruins ruggedly overlooking the North Sea, was consecrated in 1318 with Robert the Bruce present: he did seem to get about. The bishop's palace or castle nearby was, like the cathedral, regularly attacked, especially during the Reformation.

Roman Catholic Archbishop James Beaton made a Protestant martyr of divine Patrick Hamilton in 1528 and, inadvertently, ignited the tinder-box that became the Scottish Reformation. The archbishop was succeeded by his even gaudier nephew, Cardinal David Beaton, who made a martyr of the reformer George Wishart in 1546. Wishart had studied abroad with the Calvinists and, upon returning to Scotland, assisted John Knox. Thereafter the politics and theology played at St Andrews was like an illogical game of chess, with first one side winning – Cardinal Beaton was soon dispatched in his own castle – and then the other.

GLEN CLOVA

Yet again we have burning and, no doubt, looting, although you wouldn't surmise as much from this peaceful picture. Oliver Cromwell's relentless soldiers destroyed Clova Castle. Glen Clova is in Angus, close to Cortachy which, in its turn, is near Kirriemuir where J. M. Barrie (1860–1937) was born. His house, a veritable shrine to the world of *Peter Pan*, is managed by the National Trust for Scotland. In it is a letter from Captain Robert Falcon Scott written to Barrie, his godfather, from the Antarctic.

Scott and Edward Wilson stayed near Glen Clova as they planned their expedition to the South Pole in 1912. They are commemorated by a fountain. A change from a wooden seat, anyway.

BEN LOMOND

Ben Lomond (3,192 feet) is the
country's most southern 'Munro',
being midway down Loch Lomond
on the eastern shore. Loch Lomond
is, possibly, Scotland's most vulgar and
tritely romantic loch. Like most people,
I find it irresistible. The legend of Loch
Lomond is fanned by the Jacobite song
'The Bonnie Banks o' Loch Lomond',
and the fact that its proximity to the
outskirts of Glasgow makes it easy
to visit.

'Munros' are the 238 Scottish hills
and mountains not lower than 3,000
feet above sea level. They are named
after Sir Hugh Munro (1856–1919),
who defined them in 1891. Munro
climbed all but two of the peaks for
which he provided a generic noun.
The first man to scale every one was
A. E. Robertson in 1901, admittedly
a fairly obscure piece of information
but one with which to impress your
climbing friends.

Grampian

THE RIVER SPEY

The Spey, which crosses Inverness-shire, Morayshire and Banffshire, is approximately 100 miles long, making it the second-longest river in the country. It is surrounded by ravishing scenery, and fishermen smack their lips when contemplating the salmon. On its banks are whisky distilleries.

Here is a line of holiday chalets, more accurately that than beach huts, because they are not by the sea. I rather resent edifices such as these, as from the ground if not the air, they close off a part of the landscape and riverscape from the individual's eye, whether he or she be a visitor or a resident in the area. They are also not the most elegant of constructions. Solitariness is one thing, but to seek one's solitude with others of a similar inclination crowded onto one's doorstep is surely perverse.

Am I wrong to detect a touch of menace in the hidden, undisclosed silence of these photographs?

80

SPEY BAY

The Spey, cutting through three regions, is best thought of for its scenery (that is, the 'scenery' around its 100-mile length, and the river itself). It isn't an *important* river in the sense that communities, counties, countries depend upon it; although those living near it do. The Spey adds to the pleasure and mystery of being alive, simply because it is so beautiful.

And it has two other glories, not to be disregarded. First, the most succulent salmon are conjured from its waters; succulent, that is, on the understanding – which isn't always there – that they're cooked to a turn by someone who knows what she or he is doing. Second, your fish may be washed down, or remembered, with a Speyside malt whisky, which are (almost) legion. You'll have to read the appendix of Roddy Martine's comprehensive *Scotland: The Land and the Whisky* for a full list but they include: Glen Grant, Glenfarclas, Glenfiddich, Glenlivet – sorry, *The* Glenlivet – Knockando (one of my favourites) and (that definite, arrogant article again) The Macallan, regularly advertised in the national press with the best copy of any British product or institution.

What makes these malt whiskies so special? The waters of the River Spey.

RUTHVEN BARRACKS, NEAR KINGUSSIE

First, some pronunciation. 'Ruthven' is pronounced 'Riven', and 'Kingussie' is pronounced 'Kin-youssie'.

You'd not assume as much from these two somewhat austere photographs of Ruthven Barracks, but Kingussie, on the banks of the upper River Spey, is a popular tourist centre with golf, skiing at Aviemore, pony-trekking, a wildlife park at Kincraig and, for all I know, canoeing.

Kingussie was established in the late eighteenth century by the then Duke of Gordon. Ruthven is just across the Spey from Kingussie, where the Comyn family (rivals to Robert the Bruce) had a castle and where these fierce barracks stand.

James 'Ossian' Macpherson was born in Ruthven, and once taught at the school there. Famous people have to be born somewhere.

84

THE A9 JUST SOUTH OF PORTORMIN BY DUNBEATH

One of Scotland's most gentle, ruminative novelists, Neil M. Gunn (1891–1973) was born in Dunbeath, and wrote about growing up there, in his finest novel, *Morning Tide*. Dunbeath is a fishing port which participated in the herring industry, and Gunn's novel smacks of that, and of the sea.

This photograph, though, is of a road (the A9) just south of Portormin, by Dunbeath, Caithness.

THE CAIRNGORMS

The Cairngorms are probably the best-loved mountains in Britain, and it's funny to those of us who aren't obsessive mountaineers how mountains can be loved. They are the highest mass of mountains in the Grampians, in Scotland, in the UK, always remembering to exclude the solitary peak of Ben Nevis. They occupy approximately 300 square miles, which is a lot of mountain, a lot of rock, a lot of tumbling river, a lot of green and purple Highland scenery.

The sensible, not too experienced climber, can pad about on the slopes, and for the not too energetic there are chair-lifts to the ski-runs. Six of the Cairngorm summits are over 4,000 feet.

When someone says 'Cairngorm' to me, I think of the hard amber Cairngorm stone, reddish rock crystal used for adorning brooches, dirks and sporrans.

85

Highland

SOUTH OF INVERNESS

Scotland, if not the government in London, loves the railways. The West Highland line, running north to Oban and with the best scenic route of any railway line in the UK, was reprieved from closure in September 1995 as a result of a vocal national rising. The authorities, who had claimed the line was running at a loss, did not have the nerve to axe it. Among other things, it was generally agreed that the existence of the line was one of the best-kept secrets in Britain: how can trains be full if people do not know about them?

The railway system in Scotland is, as I write, administered by Scotrail, and it extends to 1,674 miles of track.

Coal mining encouraged the construction of early railways, more properly known as wagonways. The first was laid out between Tranent and Cockenzie in East Lothian in 1722. At the beginning of the nineteenth century, there was a shift from wagonways being employed as a means of industrial transport to railways as a means of public transport, enabling people – whether for work or play – to traverse their own country. The invention of the steam locomotive (James Watt from Greenock playing the fundamental role in this development) speeded up this transition. Around 1816, the Kilmarnock and Troon Railway in Ayrshire was the first in Scotland to experiment with steam. The Edinburgh and Glasgow Railway opened in 1842, and the first line to cross the Border, between Edinburgh and Berwick-upon-Tweed, in 1846. By the 1860s the Scottish rail network as it is today was virtually complete.

Until 1923 the railways were run by five companies: North British; Caledonian; Glasgow and South Western; Highland; and Great Northern of Scotland. And now the somewhat lethargic stability of British Rail and Scotrail is shortly to give way to a new division of the railway kingdom.

NEAR LOCH DUNTELCHAIG
Large areas of the Highlands are blessed or sullied, subject to your view, with pine forests. The Forestry Commission is a UK government department founded in 1919. Half the UK's forestry is in Scotland, and the Commission's headquarters are in Edinburgh.

In 1992 Scottish Natural Heritage was established by the National Heritage (Scotland) Act of the previous year. Its purposes and aims are to secure the conservation and enhancement of the natural heritage of the country, and to foster understanding of it.

Let us hope that such bodies as the Forestry Commission and Natural Heritage working in concert with, no doubt, innumerable other bureaucratic bodies will indeed enhance the environment. As Roger Crofts, chief executive of Scottish Natural Heritage, has written: 'Our identity is very much defined by our title: "Scottish" in the sense that we are a Scottish body taking Scottish action for the Scottish people; "Natural" in the sense of deriving from nature. We recognize, of course, that most of Scotland has been influenced by man over the last 5,000 years to a greater or lesser extent. So "Natural" is not a strict or restricting term: it has to embrace the concept of people in the environment.'

Difficult to do that when, without compass or map, you're trying to fight your way out of some unenchanted forest.

89

90

GLEN ROY NATIONAL NATURE RESERVE

Glen Roy, known as 'the valley of the red river' – is it blood, or sandstone? – is famous for its natural phenomenon of the Parallel Roads. A car park gives visitors access to a viewpoint which offers the best view. The Parallel Roads resemble three grassy paths running parallel (you guessed) along the mountains on both sides of the valley. Legend has it, as often it does, that they were the work of the mythical hero, Fingal. More mundanely, they are gravel ledges or terraces indicating the levels of the loch that filled the glen during the last ice age, the water being held captive by a huge glacier. When the water level diminished, new 'roads' formed, the top one being the oldest.

In 1992, the Countryside Commission and the Nature Conservancy Council merged to become the equally pompous sounding Scottish National Heritage, and it is this body which designates and manages the country's nature reserves. The first to be established was at Beinn Eighe in Wester Ross, the largest is the Cairngorms. Public access is allowed except where it might be incompatible with conservation of wildlife.

The most 'famous' Scottish nature reserve is probably Loch Garten, Speyside, managed by the Royal Society for the Protection of Birds, where in 1954 ospreys ostentatiously returned to breed. Every year ornithologists and newspapers get very excited about all this, and security is strict to protect the breeding ospreys from vandals and thieves of birds' eggs. Other wildlife here includes the miraculous capercaillie, 'the horse of the woods'; blackcock and crossbills; and red squirrels and majestic deer.

STRATH MASHIE

Jason Hawkes described the picture on the left here as 'Spire in Strath Mashie'. Seen from the air I might have described it as some alien object, perhaps trying to take over a particularly exotic area of the Highlands.

I wondered at first if it was a cairn – a heap of stones raised by climbers as a landmark on a mountain top, as if denying the summit its own dignity – but it is surely a trig-point. I can find 'trig-point' in no dictionary but the *Shorter Oxford English Dictionary* defines 'trigonometrical' in part as 'T.survey, a survey of a country or region performed by triangulation and t.calculation.' I hope you are both impressed and enlightened.

The river oozing and meandering away in the background of each photograph is the River Mashie which joins the Spey just west of Laggan.

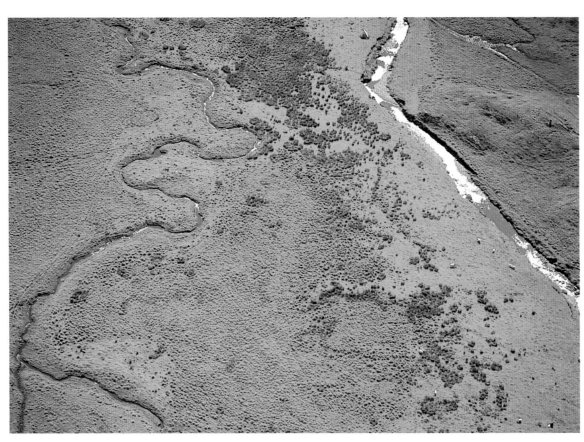

94

LOCH LAGGAN

Everyone has his or her favourite lochs.
Queen Victoria was much taken with
Loch Laggan when, on one of her first
visits to the Highlands (instructively
described in her journals), she lodged
at Ardverikie House, built by the Duke
of Abercorn in 1840, on the southern
shore. The rain, though, was too much
for her – it poured every day of her
visit – and as a result she looked
further east, fancying Balmoral estate,
which she bought in 1853. Ardverikie
House looks like the kind of grand
Scottish Victorian establishment which
by now will have been turned into
a ridiculously expensive hotel where
no one will dare complain about
the service or the prices. Instead,
and long may this be so, it remains
in private hands.

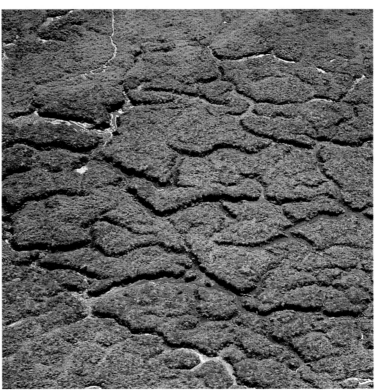

LOCH LAGGAN

Loch Laggan is at the headwaters of the River Spean. It harbours, as do so many major lochs now, its own hydroelectric dam. Scotland, with its torrential rainfall (we try to forget it in a good summer) and high mountains, is well suited to hydroelectric power production. It is still a thrill to come across hydroelectric installations in the Highlands – reservoirs, pipes linking the reservoirs to the generating stations high above the lochs, tailraces pouring water from the turbines back into lochs or rivers. The noise of the water tends to be so deafening that landscape and everyday life are temporarily blotted out.

I've always been sceptical about the existence of Nessie, the Loch Ness monster, but plainly the beast in the photograph below is the Loch Laggan monster.

BALBLAIR

The spiritual history of Scotland is almost spanned by these two photographs. Balblair is a village with a pier and Ferry Inn built in 1835. It had one of numerous ferries which crossed the Cromarty Firth to Invergordon and was still being used thirty years ago. Near to Balblair a Pictish Christian burial site was recently excavated. The poor church in the picture on the left is obviously a later building, with many of those who worshipped in it lying under the sod, beneath the flat gravestones. Did the church need to lose its roof? It was probably Roman Catholic once but, come the Reformation, used by the Church of Scotland.

Certainly the oil tanks in the other photograph have not lost their roofs, or hats, or tops. Yet their future, if and when the oil in the North Sea near to Cromarty Firth yields no more, may be infinitely shorter than that of the dignified, dying church.

Balblair is also the name of a Highland malt whisky made by Allied Distillers, bottled at five and ten years, with a fragrance of smoke and sweetness.

100

RIGS IN THE MORAY AND CROMARTY FIRTHS

In 1967, the first oil well was drilled and in 1970 the first major find was in the Forties Field (240 million tonnes) 100 miles off Aberdeen. Oil has become Scotland's hottest property – not forgetting whisky – and indeed has fuelled the clamour for Scottish nationalism and independence: why should the English have a part of our fortuitous find? That has been the cry, without much reciprocal questioning as to why 'England' should continue to feed, both financially and in kind, the northern part of Britain from the common, national coffers.

The Brent Field (off Shetland, producing 229 million tonnes) was discovered in 1971. The cost of mining oil from deep, deep down in the dark ocean initially made North Sea oil almost an indulgence, an insurance against the possible termination of supplies from elsewhere, mainly the Middle East. Come the OPEC price war of 1973–4, the North Sea suddenly became competitive. Further exploitation became a priority if self-sufficiency (whether Scotland's or the UK's) was to be achieved.

Exploration peaked in 1975, with 80 wells drilled and 27 'significant' oil and gas finds. Since then, though no one likes to noise it abroad, the pace of exploration has seriously slowed.

Production now stands at 90 million tonnes per annum. The UK is rated fifth among the oil-producing nations.

Aberdeen in particular has benefited from the bonanza of North Sea oil. It is the country's oil capital, with one of the busiest heliports in the world and more two-car families than anywhere comparable. Houses were and are again bought and sold for exotic prices, and the men from the rigs spend fortunes – the risks involved in mining oil are such that the wages paid to those on the rigs approach kings' ransoms – in Aberdeen.

In 1993 the UK's off-shore oil and gas supply industry was the world's second largest. The North Sea industry as a whole was reckoned to provide work for 300,000 people. As long ago as 1981 it was estimated that North Sea oil and gas were contributing more than 4 per cent to the UK's GDP.

The rigs, viewed from close up or afar, are modern cathedrals, cathedrals dedicated to technology and the proper exploitation of the planet's natural resources. However long we worship at them, long may they sustain us.

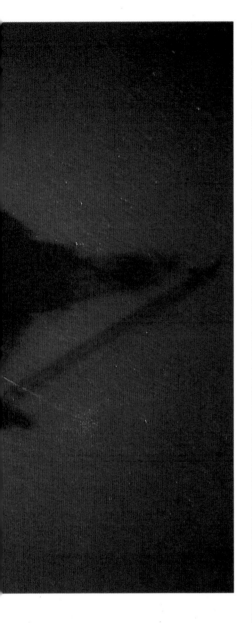

THE MORAY FIRTH

Here are dolphins disporting themselves in the Moray Firth, and a smile crosses your face at the thought. The Firth is one of the main areas in UK waters for dolphins, porpoises and whales: herds of 20 to 30 animals can sometimes be seen during the summer months. The dolphins appear playful, and can often be seen leaping out of the water. Bottlenose dolphins are the species most often seen from the coast. White-beaked and Risso's dolphins are more likely to be encountered further out at sea.

The Moray Firth bottlenose dolphins represent one of only two or three resident populations known to exist in UK waters, and the only one, as far as is known, in the North Sea. More than 100 dolphins are thought to be living in the Firth.

Adults have beaks and tall, sickle-shaped dorsal fins which curve backwards. They are between 3.1 and 3.8 metres in length, and weigh between 180 and 300 kilograms. They live for around 25 years, although bottlenose dolphins aged 50 have been noted. Females reach sexual maturity between the ages of five and twelve, and often give birth to a single calf every two to three years.

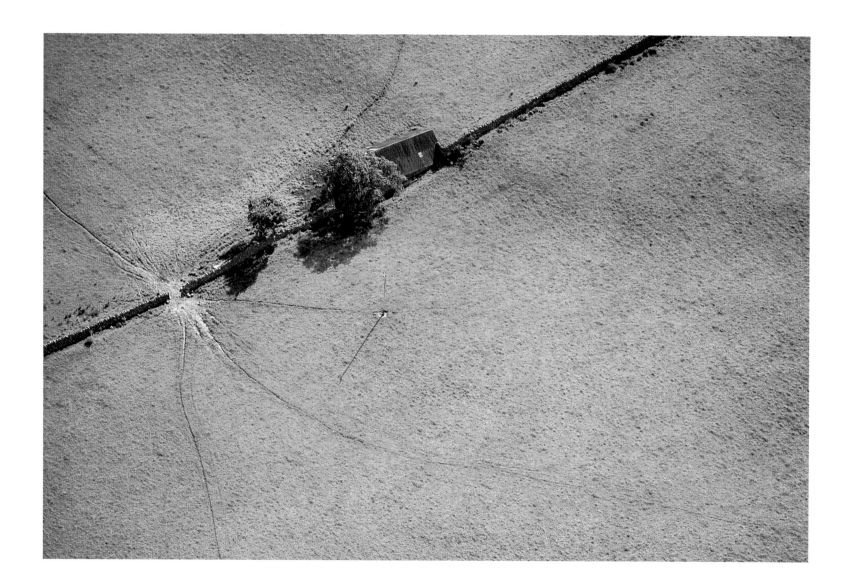

104

THE BLACK ISLE

If I'd taken this picture would Jason Hawkes have agreed to write a caption? I doubt it.

The photograph happens to have been taken on the Black Isle – which, in a perverse Scottish way, is neither an island nor black – south of Munlochy Bay, if you wish to check up if the break in the wall has been repaired.

It's a daring photograph, of solitary longing, of the end of civilization, of a farmer (or landlord) having run out of money. More mundanely, note the footpath, the tread of all too many people taking a short cut, from somewhere to somewhere.

Dry stane dykes are very much a part of Scotland's geography and discipline, the right of individuals to demarcate their land, and thus their lives. Here that is broken, a hiatus. I once saw the Prince of Wales repairing a dry stane dyke, replacing the stones. Everyone is at it.

FYRISH MONUMENT

At first glance you may have thought that the dramatic stone temple in the foreground was of some famous Celtic site. In fact Fyrish Monument – three miles east of Alness, just north of Cromarty Firth – is a near replica of the gateway to Negapatnam in south India. This town was held by the Dutch when captured in 1781 by General Sir Hector Munro of Novar in Ross and Cromarty, who had commanded the Gordon Highlanders when they were dispatched, as the 89th Regiment of Foot, to India in 1760.

In 1768 Munro was returned to the House of Commons as MP for Inverness Burghs. He held the seat for 34 years, but this didn't stop him returning to India, where he cut swaths, winning battles until the humiliation of the Battle of Polilur in 1780, which he and another Scot, Colonel Baillie, were all too responsible for losing.

The Fyrish Monument, which may have been built as a private act of penance by Munro, was created to provide work at a time of poverty, famine and unemployment in the area.

105

AVIEMORE

Aviemore sprung into being as a Highland sweatshop in the 1960s, before which it had been a nondescript little place; a railway station on the way to Inverness.

In the 1960s it became the Highlands' first purpose-built holiday resort. It is fashionable for skiing with a mass of hotels, hostels, chalets and caravans. There are conference centres, leisure centres and health centres.

I suppose it had to happen.

INVERNESS

'This castle hath a pleasant seat, the air/Nimbly and sweetly recommends itself/Unto our gentle senses', said Shakespeare's King Duncan when he arrived as a guest at Macbeth's castle at Inverness. He was right about the climate but otherwise he didn't know what was going to hit him.

Inverness is still the 'capital of the Highlands' as Dr Johnson called it, but little remains of its historic past. It is sited most strategically, north of Loch Ness, defence being its primary requirement until the eighteenth century. It's a douce enough town, but I remember being deeply disappointed the first time I visited it by its smallness and lack of character. I had expected it to be close in population to Aberdeen (200,000) or Dundee (165,000), but Inverness has only about 36,000 inhabitants.

But let me not be unkind about it. The opening of the Caledonian Canal in 1822 and the advance of the railways in the latter half of the nineteenth century made inevitable Inverness's place as the commercial and administrative town of the Highlands and as the principal resort, and so it remains.

108

CAMPING BY THE AIRD

This is a Boy Scouts' campsite just
west of Inverness. William Smith
rarely receives credit for it, but in
1883, twenty-five years before Baden-
Powell started the Scouts, Smith
founded in Glasgow the Boys' Brigade.
Its object was 'the advancement of
God's kingdom among Boys and the
promotion of habits of Reverence,
Discipline, Self-Respect, and all
that tends towards a true Christian
Manliness'. Very John Knox.

FORT GEORGE

Fort George, which stands elegantly
on a promontory sticking out into the
Moray Firth near Ardersier, nine miles
east of Inverness, is named after King
George II. It was built between 1747
and 1770 as a direct response to the
second Jacobite rising.

I have spent a week within its walls,
surrounded by sea on three sides. One
year in the late 1950s the Edinburgh
Academy Combined Cadet Force
annual summer camp took place here,
and how preferable the place was to
other ghastly camps visited, mostly in
Yorkshire. The food was rather grim,
I recall, but young cadets, a few years
before National Service was done away
with, shouldn't be too coddled.

The essential *Collins Encyclopaedia
of Scotland* quotes Dr Johnson (the
fort was completed three years before
Johnson and Boswell made their
journey north) as proclaiming
Fort George to be 'the most regular
fortification in the island'. It remains
so, its defences never having been
attacked. Of the architecture, the
Encyclopaedia finely opines: 'With sea
on three sides its polygonal ramparts
have four bastions commanding the
seaward approaches but reserve the full
Vaubanesque vocabulary of ravelins,
lunettes, etc for the landward approach
to the east.'

So there.

111

LOCH NESS

If you were to list the 'top' Scottish tourist attractions, they would certainly include that mythical beast (but not one known to heraldry), the Loch Ness Monster. I assume it's mythical but you can get yourself into a great deal of trouble if you assert as much to believers. Maybe our photographer has taken as many photographs of Loch Ness as he has in the hope that someone will spot the monster in one of his pictures.

Like most lochs, it has little tufts of islands upon it; land reclaimed from water to water failing to conquer land. And boats, whether for work or pleasure, busily bustling about.

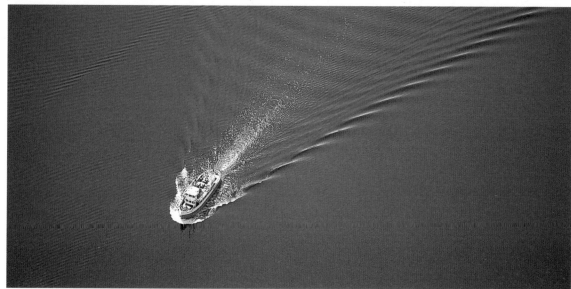

LOCH NESS

Loch Ness is twenty-three miles long, on average a mile wide, and exceptionally deep, hence the belief that Nessie, as the monster is affectionately known, can lodge below without being discovered. In places, Loch Ness is thought to be as much as 1,000 feet deep.

It is, not forgetting the more romantic and more southerly Loch Lomond, the classic Highland loch. It is the central feature of the Great Glen, mountains rising dramatically on both sides. It is so regular that in this picture it looks like a wide canal.

113

CASTLE URQUHART

There are castles and castles in Scotland but Urquhart is one of the most interesting, though little of its structure remains. It stands on a headland to the south of Glen Urquhart, and looks up and down Loch Ness (assuming castles have eyes). Indeed, down the centuries it has been a most important strategic fortification. Robert the Bruce captured it in 1308 – following Edward I's death in 1307 the English were ejected from the country and all the great castles (except Berwick and Stirling) were recovered by the Scots. During the fifteenth century the Lords of the Isles filched it from the Scottish king and it wasn't recaptured until 1509 when James IV bequeathed the lordship to John Grant of Freuchie (who he, indeed). During the seventeenth century, Covenanters in 1645 and Jacobites in 1689 staked their claims for the stronghold. It was in part blown up in 1691 and thereafter quickly began to disintegrate.

Such is the fate of castles; but by their very nature they bring destruction upon themselves.

Charles Maclean, in his *Romantic Scotland*, remarks of Castle Urquhart that 'there are two hidden vaults, one of which is said to contain treasure, the other, the plague, kept magically bottled there until it shall be needed again'. Let us hope he doesn't know something we don't.

THE FALLS OF FOYERS

In the eighteenth and early nineteenth centuries the Falls of Foyers, on the south side of Loch Ness, were much admired by writers and other travellers. Dr Johnson growled about their 'dreadful depth' (had he fallen in?), Robert Burns penned some couplets to their 'mossy floods'. Christopher North (1785–1854), the Paisley-born author, editor and friend of Wordsworth and other Lakeland writers, waxed lyrical about the Falls, 'the most magnificent cataract . . . in Britain . . . worth walking a thousand miles to behold'.

Today the waterfall is by no means as romantic or, indeed, as gushing as it was since it has been harnessed to Scotland's first hydroelectric scheme, opened as long ago as 1896. British Aluminium closed the plant in 1967 but a power station continues to purloin water from the once mighty Falls of Foyers.

FORT AUGUSTUS

'Augustus' is hardly the first Scottish name one thinks of. The small town at the southern end of Loch Ness is named after William Augustus, Duke of Cumberland, colloquially known as 'Butcher' Cumberland because of the swaths he cut through the Highlands and Highlanders after the Jacobite defeat at Culloden. The fort and barracks were built by General Wade, he of the network of military roads, in 1730.

The fort itself was sold in 1867 to Lord Lovat, descendant of an executed Jacobite (and of course a Roman Catholic). He gave the building to the Benedictine order which opened it as a school in 1878. It remains Scotland's premier Catholic boarding school.

What a site on which to be educated and to learn the harsh complexities of Scotland's history, combining religion and politics, if they aren't one and the same anyway.

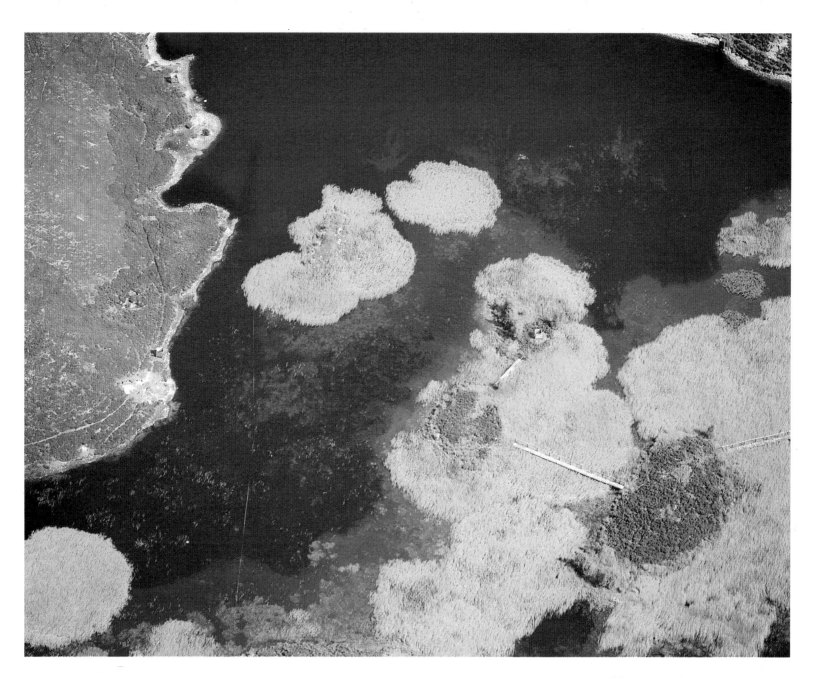

**NORTH OF LOCH
DUNTELCHAIG, BY LOCH NESS**
Maybe the poor benighted monster
is below this map of a loch, having
escaped from Loch Ness to reside
elsewhere in peace.

GLEN MORISTON

Oh so regular, oh so boring, oh so neat, with the grey ribbon of road snaking through the centre. And who are we to mock or attempt to patronize?

At the beginning of the First World War, there was no public housing. By 1981, 55 per cent of UK homes were publicly owned, if not possessed. In 1990 Scotland counted for 2.1million houses of which about 920,000 were owned by local authorities. Of these, nearly 10 per cent (around 81,000) were estimated to be 'below tolerable standards'. It was a fundamental problem across the country, but was at its worst in Glasgow where the District Council, Britain's largest landlord, owned 170,000 houses.

In 1986 it set up a committee of inquiry chaired by the highly respected Professor Sir Robert Grieve. Its conclusion was that diversification of tenure, including transfer of a quarter of the District's housing stock to diverse owners, was urgently needed. Simultaneously, the Conservative government's Secretary of State for Scotland, Malcolm Rifkind, reached a similar conclusion with his Scottish Homes policy.

Now, new and refurbished homes are seeping into Scotland's cityscapes, tower blocks are being demolished (together with the reputations of certain architects and town-planning departments), and new forms of ownership, such as tenant-management co-operatives, are springing up. There is, however, a long away to go, as urban unrest and the law courts regularly attest.

IN THE HIGHLANDS

In the highlands, in the country places,
Where the old plain men have rosy faces,
And the young fair maidens
  Quiet eyes;
Where essential silence cheers and blesses,
And for ever in the hill-recesses
Her more lovely music
  Broods and dies.

O to mount again where erst I haunted;
Where the old red hills are bird-enchanted,
And the low green meadows
  Bright with sward;
And when even dies, the million-tinted,
And the night has come, and planets glinted,
Lo, the valley hollow
  Lamp-bestarred!

O to dream, O to awake and wander
There, and with delight to take and render,
Through the trance of silence,
  Quiet breath;
Lo! for there, among the flowers
 and grasses,
Only the mightier movement sounds
 and passes;
Only winds and rivers,
  Life and death.

Robert Louis Stevenson
(1850–94)

119

HEATHER BURNING

If the thistle has been the emblem of Scottish royalty and Scottish pride for 500 years, prominent in heraldry, heather has similarly been the national plant. It comes basically in purple and in white, at least to those who aren't botanists.

It grows like wildfire, and like wildfire it is ignited every year to keep it in a young, healthy condition. Heather acts as a cushion to the heaths and bogs of the eastern and central Highlands where it is particularly dominant. New heather shoots are the passion of red grouse, who gobble the shoots and then, in their time, are punctured with shot, red grouse being a much-coveted game bird.

As *Collins Encyclopaedia of Scotland* says, 'The tiny purple flowers are so numerous they can colour a whole hillside in late summer. Heather flowers are an important source of nectar for bees and, in former times, for flavouring heather ale. Among the traditional uses to which heather has been put are thatch, rope, bedding, brushes and dye.' Clearly a versatile as well as, for the Scot at least, a stirring plant.

Heather takes a leading role in Robert Louis Stevenson's *Kidnapped*; and in that novel's sequel, *David Balfour* (as *Catriona* was more aptly called in the States). A chapter is entitled 'The Heather on Fire'. But we are dealing with a metaphor, which is fine: 'The heather is on fire within my wame.' 'Wame' is Scots for belly.

FISH FARM BY THE BEAULY

The River Beauly runs from Strathglass to the Beauly Firth, west of Inverness. This is the country of the Clan Fraser of Lovat, and the photograph is of a fish farm (presumably the fish under the plastic covers in the barrels are preserved in salt or, more probably these days, ice).

Scottish fishermen, despite EC bureaucracy, continue to land about three-quarters of the UK's catch. Sea fishing has, since time immemorial, been a fundamental Scottish industry, both for consumption at home and for export. Fish and chips is still cheaper and fresher in Scotland, even the inland cities, than anywhere else in the UK.

DUNROBIN CASTLE

Now here is an improbable building, in a commanding position looking out to the North Sea, between Brora and Golspie. For 700 years the castle has been the seat of the Earls and Dukes of Sutherland (originally 'South Lands').

Dunrobin is thought to have been named after Robert, familiarly known as Robin, the 6th Earl, and is first recorded in 1401. Bits of the original building may still be seen. The present edifice, built to resemble a Loire chateau (though the weather's somewhat gustier), was concocted in the mid-nineteenth century by Sir Charles Barry.

True to the tradition of castles being blown up or set fire to, Dunrobin was accidentally set ablaze in 1915. Its most distinguished rooms were redesigned by the influential Edinburgh-born architect Sir Robert Lorimer (1864–1929) between 1914 and 1919. The castle and its pleasing gardens are open to the public.

LOCH LINNHE

Loch Linnhe lies at the feet of mighty Ben Nevis, a watery handmaiden to Britain's highest mountain. On the eastern edge of the loch is Fort William. In the loch itself, on a grassy islet, is the restored and refurbished thirteenth-century fortress, Castle Stalker, which evokes the entire history of the Highlands when seen in silhouette in the morning mists or at dusk. It is privately owned, and during the summer months its owners may be observed trying to behave as if they live in an ordinary house.

The area known as Appin touches Loch Linnhe as it flows inland to Loch Leven and Loch Eil. Readers of Robert Louis Stevenson's indispensable Highlands novel *Kidnapped* will recall the Appin murder of Colin Campbell of Glenure, a Hanoverian *apparatchik* familiarly known as 'The Red Fox' and the mystery, which remains to this day, of who killed him. Campbell was shot dead on the shores of Loch Linnhe on 14 May 1752 as retribution for evicting Stewart lairds from their homes and replacing them with Campbells. A jury of eleven Campbells and one other (why not twelve?) sentenced one James Stewart of Glen Duror to be hanged for the murder which nobody believed he'd committed.

126

THE CALEDONIAN CANAL

The Caledonian Canal, Scotland's longest at sixty miles, is a stately waterway connecting Corpath, near Fort William, with Clachnaharry, near Inverness. It is one of the country's great, early nineteenth-century engineering triumphs; Thomas Telford having devised 'Neptune's Staircase', a ladder of eight locks at Banavie.

In its passage, the Caledonian Canal embraces three lochs: Loch Lochy, Loch Oich (where it cuts through the town of Fort Augustus) and Loch Ness. When first opened in 1822 the Canal was found too shallow for many of the boats that tried to use it, and it wasn't completed until 1847. Twenty-two miles of its route are the Canal itself, the rest the water of the existing lochs.

LOCH GARRY

You would think there were enough names to go round Scotland's admittedly myriad lochs but there are two Loch Garrys (and the name is Welsh, too) one in Inverness-shire, the other in Perthshire.

Here is a litany of lochs: Loch Awe, Loch Creran, Loch Dochart, Loch Doon, Loch Earn, Loch Eil, Loch Etive, Loch Ewe, Loch Fyne, Loch Garten, Loch Inch, Loch Laggan, Loch Leven (there are two of these also: one in Argyll, one in Kinross-shire), Loch Linnhe, Loch Lochy, Loch Lomond, Loch Moidart, Loch Morar, Loch Morlich, Loch Ness, Loch Nevis, Loch Oich, Loch Rannoch, Loch Shiel, Loch Tay, Loch Voil.

These are only some of the better-known ones.

127

BEINN DHORAIN

One of the great long poems in twentieth-century Scottish literature is Iain Crichton Smith's 'Deer on the High Hills' (1961). Here are a few lines:

A deer looks through you to the
other side,
and what it is and sees is an
inhuman pride . . .

Yesterday three deer stood at the
roadside.
It was icy January and there they
were
like debutantes on a smooth
ballroom floor . . .

What is the knowledge of the deer?
Is there a philosophy of the hills?
Do their heads peer into the live
stars? . . .

There are three species of deer found in Scotland. The largest is the red deer, widespread in the Highlands and now colonizing woods in Lowland Scotland. The smallest is the roe deer, found in woodland and sometimes in large town gardens. In between is the sika deer, brought from Japan 100 years ago to adorn the parks and gardens of large houses. It soon escaped, became wild, and now infiltrates woods in many areas.

Red deer have lived in Scotland for thousands of years. They were hunted in the Stone Age and deer meat or venison has been prized ever since. They are large animals, standing up to 1.2 metres at the shoulder. They are only red-coloured during the summer months when they have a short coat suitable for warm weather. In winter they grow a longer, rougher-looking coat which can vary from dark brown to grey.

Like all Scottish deer, only the males, or stags, have antlers. These grow every year and become larger as the stag gets older. The old antlers fall off in March

and April, and start regrowing almost immediately.

Deer can live for up to twenty years, but this is unusual, most not living much beyond ten years. There are approximately 300,000 wild red deer in Scotland, and if some were not culled every year many would die of starvation. The stags are normally shot for sport; people will pay hundreds of pounds for the privilege.

BEINN DHORAIN

Is this a Munro? Yes, being over 3,000 feet, it is. Near Bridge of Orchy, Beinn Dhorain is 3,523 feet. Our nanny, while pregnant, climbed five Munros in a recent weekend, which shows – if proof is called for – that the higher Scottish mountains can be conquered without too much fuss.

Some Beinns, or Bens, are obviously more glamorous than others. Ben Nevis, Cruachan, Eighe, Lomond, Macdui are frequently cited and frequently photographed. The highest mountain, admittedly a Munro, I've ever climbed is the perversely named Loch Nagar. Visibility at the top was so bad that we 'missed the view and viewed the mist'. I felt lucky, albeit drenched, to come down alive.

129

LOCH ALSH

Here is a view of Loch Alsh, looking east to Loch Duich.

You would like the names of yet more lochs? Here are some:

Loch Clunie, Loch Coruisk, Loch Ericht, Loch Fleet, Loch Goil, Loch Hourn, Loch Ken, Loch Long, Loch Maree, Loch nan Uamh, Loch Naver, Loch Ossian, Loch Quoich, Loch Roag, Loch Ruthven, Loch Ryan, Loch Shin, Loch Sloy, Loch Stemster, Loch Sunart, Loch Sween, Loch Treig, Loch Tulla.

That's enough lochs, surely.

LOCH FLEET

One of the country's most important bird reserves is situated by Loch Fleet, just south of Golspie on the east coast of Sutherland. The variety of birdlife in the various habitat here includes redstart, goldcrest, crossbill and great northern diver, and in winter elder and long-tailed duck. Peregrine, golden eagle, merlin, buzzard, short-eared owls and sparrowhawk patrol the area, hunting over the sand dunes.

LOCH OICH

By the shores of Loch Oich near Laggan on 3 July 1544, took place the bloodiest battle fought in the Highlands. Four hundred members of the Clan Fraser stumbled upon, the way these things happen, seven hundred members of the Clans Ranald, Cameron and Donald – well, it makes a change from Campbells. Each side decided to wipe out the other, and so hot was the weather, they started by stripping to their shirts, the ensuing slaughter being known to historians as The Battle of the Shirts. By the end of the day of hacking and gouging by the lochside, it is said that only four Frasers and eight members of the opposition remained to tell the tale.

RIVER LOCHY

The Caledonian Canal passes through the Great Glen, created 420 million years ago by a geological fault which split Scotland in two. The glen contains Loch Ness, Loch Oich and the soothingly named Loch Lochy.

As James Campbell comments in his witty and instructive text to *The Aerofilms Book of Scotland from the Air*, 'By Gairlochy, where Loch Lochy meets River Lochy, is Loch Lochy Lock. Try saying that after a dram of Dufftown malt.'

133

LOCH CLUNIE

Here we look east. The Castle of Clunie stands on a tiny island in the loch. It was the boyhood home of the brilliant young James Crichton (1560–82), later to be known as 'The Admirable Crichton', killed in a brawl while in the service of the Duke of Mantua. Reputedly great scholar, poet, linguist and swordsman, he is not to be confused with the butler of the same sobriquet, the eponymous hero of J. M. Barrie's 1902 comedy.

134

CHURCH NEAR BRORA

The Times for 28 September 1995
announced, in black headlines:
'Scotland turns its back on the church'.
Reports in the Scottish press were
more circumspect. However, a report
just released indicated that church
attendance in Scotland was declining
at the rate of a congregation a week.
Churches of all denominations would
be empty by 2044 if the trend
continued.

Church attendance remains strongest
in the Western Isles, at 39 per cent
of the adult population. It is lowest in
Aberdeen, with 8 per cent of adults
turning up to worship God rather than
the god of the oil boom.

The Church of Scotland is worst
hit. In no area is it showing growth.
Roman Catholic attendance is growing
in the Western Isles, Skye, Orkney,
Aberdeen (surprisingly) and the
Borders but declining elsewhere.

NEAR BRORA

You wouldn't know it from this dramatic picture of sea, coast and road but Brora gives pride of place to a whisky distillery: Clynelish. The truth is that many places in the northern Highlands do. United Distillers own the plant at which whisky is bottled at fourteen years of age. The taste is quite peaty, mature with a slightly dry finish.

The point of whisky from Scotland is that it reflects the climate of the country, its water and its people. Easy to say; difficult, unless you have the secret of the distilling, to realize in the bottle. Although whisky has been distilled in the Highlands for more than 500 years, it was after the Jacobite defeat at Culloden Moor in 1746 that production of the nippy beverage became the means by which Highlanders could pay the rent.

Many distillers welcome visitors interested in learning about the processes by which whisky is distilled. They will not, however, impart to you the recipes which result in the unique taste of their own malt whiskies.

136

WATERFALL IN BADENOCH

From scenes like these old Scotia's grandeur springs,
That makes her loved at home, revered abroad;
Princes and lords are but the breath of kings,
An honest man's the noblest work of God.

The Jolly Beggars
Robert Burns (1759–96)

FORT WILLIAM

If truth be told, Fort William is not a town of much excitement. Despite its lovely location at the head of Loch Linnhe and the entrance to the Great Glen, it has little to offer culturally, architecturally or otherwise. Fort William suffers torrential rain every year, built, as it is, in the shadow of Ben Nevis. Cromwell's General Monk built the original fort, calling it Inverlochy. It was renamed in 1690, after William III, when it was expanded.

To me, Fort William is simply a destination of the West Highland Railway from Glasgow, and to Glasgow from London, Euston. This railway crosses and embraces landscape which rivals that seen from the Orient Express travelling from London, Waterloo to Venice, and is a darn sight cheaper. It is probably the most romantic railway journey in the world.

In 1995 British Rail announced it was killing the 94-year-old service as too few people were using it. This led to a most unholy row and within a few months the service was reinstated, if only so that peers of the realm might use the sleeper from London and travel in some style and peace to their grouse moors. As I write, British Rail, never a body to treat defeat lightly, is intending to reduce the Fort William sleeper to only one carriage. Under the terms of an agreement reached in September 1995, the three north Scottish sleeper trains serving Inverness, Aberdeen and Fort William, have been amalgamated into one 16-carriage train. The train is broken up at Edinburgh in the wee hours of the morning, with six sleepers going to Inverness, four to Aberdeen and, at present, two to Fort William.

The reason the London to Fort William service was so little used was because it was one of British Rail's best-kept secrets: too few people knew about it. Now that they do, there is great demand to book its 42 beds. Why not put on more sleeper coaches? British Rail explained that the sheer length of the train meant that no extra carriages could be laid on for the Fort William service, despite the demand, because platforms at Euston could take only sixteen carriages.

No suggestion, you'll note, that a platform might be extended.

EMBO BEACH

Embo is north of Dornoch, south of Golspie and has Dunrobin Castle north of it on the open Sutherland coast. Here we see that habitual visual monstrosity which pervades the British coast, a humourless regiment of trailer caravans with, frequently, their denizens' motor cars tucked uncosily in next to them.

And yet the revenue these holidaymakers provide is, of course, a godsend to the local community.

The creamy waves, though, look disconcerted by the coastal fortifications.

NEAR LOTHBEG POINT

A solitary caravan, with accompanying car. That, it is hard to object to. A family, probably, enjoying being on the edge of the land, next to sand and sea.

I've never camped in a caravan. One of the most ominous nights I've spent, however, was under canvas at Glencoe. You feel hemmed in by the universe, by the bloody weight of Scotland's past. No wonder the Scots cannot get the massacre of the MacDonalds by the Campbells in 1692 out of their collective psyche.

**Looking north
from Lybster**

More Burns, this time from
'My Heart's in the Highlands':

> *My heart's in the Highlands, my
> heart's not here;
> My heart's in the Highlands
> a-chasing the deer;
> Chasing the wild deer, and
> following the roe,
> My heart's in the Highlands,
> wherever I go.*

and, for good measure, the novelist
John Galt (1779–1839), born in Irvine,
Ayrshire:

> *From the lone shieling of the misty
> island
> Mountains divide us, and the waste
> of seas –
> Yet still the blood is strong, the
> heart is Highland,
> And we in dreams behold the
> Hebrides.*

142

SCOTTISH COASTLINE

Instead of facts and opinions, you'd now like some statistics. Me too.

The Central Statistics Unit of The Scottish Office (let's keep it light) reports that the total area of Scotland is 30,418 square miles. Of that, the land area is 29,761 and inland water, notably lochs, is 657. Given that from tip to toe the length of Scotland is approximately 250 miles, the total mainland coastline is an astonishing 2,427 miles. This includes the islands. The main coastlines of the Orkneys, Shetlands and the Western Isles total 587 miles. In addition, the coastlines of the smaller islands in Highland Region total 508 miles and 835 in Strathclyde Region.

143

HARVESTING

The harvest is in for another year,
thank God. The stookies (haystacks)
are laid out, as if in abstract paintings,
across the fields. In one photograph,
late-afternoon shadows begin to seep
or smear across the field; the canvas.

In 1786 Scotland's national poet,
Robert Burns, celebrated, in 'Corn
Riggs', a night less on the tiles than
in the fields:

It was upon a Lammas night
When corn riggs* are bonie,
Beneath the moon's unclouded light,
I held awa to Annie:
The time flew by, wi' tentless* heed,
Till 'tween the late and early;
Wi' sma' persuasion she agreed,
To see me thro' the barley.

The sky was blue, the wind was still,
The moon was shining clearly;
I set her down, wi' right good will,
Amang the rigs of barley:
I ken't her heart wa a' my ain;
I lov'd her most sincerely;
I kiss'd her owre and owre agin,
Amang the rigs o' barley.

Corn rigs, an' barley rigs,
An' corn rigs are bonie:
I'll ne'er forget that happy night,
Amang the rigs wi' Annie.

*riggs: fields
*tentless: careless

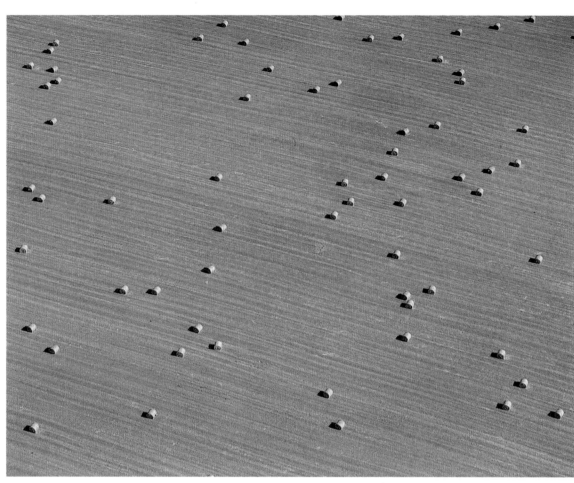

SALMON FARMING IN SCALPAY

There are salmon in all Scottish river systems except for a few streams which run directly to the sea. The main Scottish watershed runs north–south, much of it close to the country's west coast. Almost all the large rivers therefore flow to the east. In the larger systems, salmon may come in from the sea every month of the year but in the smaller rivers, runs are usual only in summer and autumn. The larger rivers – including the Tweed, the Tay, the Spey and the Dee – are world famous for salmon.

In his *Salmon Fisheries in Scotland* (1991), Robert Williamson writes: 'The general life history of the salmon is well known and need not be repeated here; but one point is specially relevant to the recent management of the Scottish fisheries and is worth emphasis: a salmon returns to its native river to spawn.' Sadly, pollution is taking its toll on the fish, as is netting at sea and, indeed, salmon farming on catches in lochs and rivers all over the country.

But we are inordinately proud of the fish. *Chambers Dictionary* describes it as 'a large, highly esteemed fish, with silvery sides'.

Salmon may frequently be observed leaping, turning and twisting up from sparkling streams, and it's instructive to watch it climbing the salmon ladder attached to the dam of the hydroelectric plant at Pitlochry.

The bad news is that it's become so common and relatively inexpensive in restaurants that its flavour appears to have become bland. It is served succulently, though, at the Vintner's Room, a magnificent restaurant in Edinburgh's port of Leith.

146

THE HEBRIDES

In the Highlands, the midges – hellish Scottish mosquitoes – are, during the summer, the main topic of conversation, or at least the introduction to a conversation. Elsewhere a mention of 'the weather' is *de rigueur*, the assumption being that it is appalling. Yet, in practice this is less and less true: the summer of 1995 was another idyllic, almost seamless one, the sun and blue skies smiling on the landscape, leading, of course, to anxieties that the crops would suffer.

The west coast has the highest annual rainfall, but only in the heights. Ben Nevis garners twice as many annual inches of rain as Fort William, a mere four miles away. The prevailing westerly winds bring the warmth of the Gulf Stream, hence the lush vegetation in western glens and sea lochs. Scotland's eastern seaboard is both drier and cooler. The Cairngorms – Aberdeenshire, Inverness-shire and Banffshire – suffer more snow than the mountains of the west, and snow may lie all year in the north-facing corries of Ben Wyvis above Cromarty Firth. Clan Munro's tenure of the vicinity included, believe it or not, payment of one snowball to the monarch each time he passed.

147

THE ISLAND OF SKYE

To me, Skye is the bleakest, at least most austere, island of them all. Yet it is a fundamental area of the 'Highlands and Islands', and covering 535 square miles it is no blot on the seascape. Besides which, my parents first met there; and Bonnie Prince Charlie, bless him, hid in a cave there after he'd picked up his skirts and fled from the disaster of Culloden Moor.

As Robert Louis Stevenson put it (1896):

> *Sing me a song of a lad that is gone,*
> *Say, could that lad be I?*
> *Merry of soul he sailed on a day*
> *Over the sea to Skye.*

And James Hogg (1770–1835), author of the archetypal and greatest of all Scottish novels, *The Private Memoirs and Confessions of a Justified Sinner* (1824):

> *We'll o'er the water, we'll o'er*
>   *the sea,*
> *We'll o'er the water to Charlie;*
> *Come weel, come wo, we'll gather*
>   *and go,*
> *And live or die wi' Charlie.*

And what matter if he was thinking of the Jacobite prince back in France?

The Cuillins, the mighty mountains to the south of the island, present some of the most thrilling rock climbing in the UK, and on Skye there are no fewer than fifteen peaks which count as 'Munros'. The island has always drawn writers and artists to it, and among those who have limned it, in word or in line, are Thomas Gray, Samuel Johnson, Sir Walter Scott (*The Lord of the Isles*), and J. M. W. Turner.

150

THE ISLAND OF SKYE

Skye remains very much central to
Gaelic culture, and many of its nearly
10,000 inhabitants speak Gaelic in
everyday lives. Yet Skye is hardly
isolated from the mainland: five ferry
terminals connect it to the mainland
and other islands. In the summer,
a bewildering one million tourists
(although they mostly would think of
themselves as more than a cut above
the pejorative 'tourists') visit the
island, hitherto mostly reaching it
by MacBrayne's ferry from Kyle of
Lochalsh on the mainland. Crofting
and fishing remain Skye's fundamental
activities, as they've been for centuries,
but tourism is increasingly crucial to
the island's economy.

There are likely to be many more
visitors since on 16 October 1995 the

island of Skye – called by Sorley Maclean, the Gaelic poet, 'the great beautiful bird of Scotland' – was, for the first time, welded to the mainland of the country. As Magnus Linklater, previously editor of *The Scotsman* and now columnist for *The Times*, put it: 'It is no longer an island. Joined to the mainland by a concrete box-girder bridge, Skye has become an adjunct rather than an entity. Now it will be possible to drive across in just a few minutes. The days when you dipped down from the pier at Kyle of Lochalsh, bounded up a ramp onto the ferry, then swung out into the teeth of a southwesterly gale tearing up from the Sound of Sleat, are over. The MacBrayne's ferry is being withdrawn to force motorists to use the bridge and pay the tolls.'

It costs a preposterous £5.20 (£4.30 in winter) to cross the 570-metre bridge, making it the highest toll in Europe. To add insult to ugliness, even before the official opening (Charles Kennedy, MP for Skye, declined to attend) cracks were revealed in the concrete of the £24 million structure. It is questionable who benefits from a bridge which, it has to be said, doesn't have the same kind of purpose as the road bridges crossing the Forth and the Tay. As Magnus Linklater has written, 'Skye is not just any island, it is a Hebridean dream, an inspiration, a state of mind.'

151

152

RIVER DRYNOCK, SKYE

On Skye, roads seem to lead nowhere, and people are infrequently in evidence. I've always found it pretty barren. The mountains, notably the Cuillins, are another matter; starkly magnificent. And if you look up in the sky – the sky of Skye – you may well see golden eagles whirling and wheeling, soaring and circling.

Only about 450 pairs of golden eagle remain in Britain, most of them breeding in Scotland. They are most numerous in the Highlands and Western Isles, where they are often taken, by poets and those of a romantic disposition, as a metaphor for the untamed Highlander. Both, in a way, are protected species: the independence of the body, the freedom of the mind.

Like the Highlander during the Highland Clearances, in the nineteenth century the golden eagle was threatened with extinction owing to over-zealous sheep farmers and the self-righteous, self-confident proprietors of grouse moors. Its survival, its size (its wing span is over seven feet), and its solitary and imperial flight make it a force of nature to be wondered at.

EILEAN DONAN CASTLE

Eilean Donan (it even sounds like Debussy) is the ultimate romantic Scottish castle; like a Disney version of Camelot. I love it, whether the view from the entrance to Loch Duich or from the advertisements. Originally it was a thirteenth-century pile. It had the usual sort of history of innumerable Scottish castles. It was destroyed during the abortive Jacobite rebellion of 1719, only to be turned into its present vision 'dream castle' in the 1930s. Why mock its romantic purity?

A Scottish Reading List

BILLCLIFFE, Roger: *The Glasgow Boys* (John Murray, 1985)

BROWN, George Mackay: *An Orkney Tapestry* (Victor Gollancz, 1969)

BURNS, Robert: *Poems, Chiefly in the Scottish Dialect* (Kilmarnock edition, 1786)

CATLIN, Angela: *Natural Light: Portraits of Scottish Writers* (Paul Harris, 1985)

CAMPBELL, James: *The Aerofilms Book of Scotland from the Air* (Weidenfeld & Nicolson, 1984)

CHAMBERS SCOTS DICTIONARY, compiled by Alexander Warrack (W & R Chambers, 1911)

COCKBURN, Henry (Lord): *Memorials of His Time* (1856)

DAICHES, David: *Literature and Gentility in Scotland* (Edinburgh University Press, 1982)

DAICHES, David, Peter JONES and Jean JONES: *A Hotbed of Genius: The Scottish Enlightenment 1730–1790* (Edinburgh University Press, 1986)

DAVIE, George: *The Democratic Intellect: Scotland and her Universities in the 19th Century* (Edinburgh University Press, 1961)

DOUGLAS, George: *The House with the Green Shutters* (Thomas Nelson and Sons, 1908)

DOUGLAS, Sir George (editor): *Scottish Fairy and Folk Tales* (Walter Scott)

DUNN, Douglas (editor): *The Faber Book of Twentieth-Century Scottish Poetry* (1992)

DUVAL, K. D. and Sydney Goodsir SMITH (editors): *Hugh MacDiarmid: a festschrift* (K. D. Duval, 1962)

FITZGIBBON, Theodora: *Traditional Scottish Cooking* (Fontana, 1980)

FRASER, Antonia: *Mary, Queen of Scots* (Weidenfeld & Nicolson, 1969)

FRASER, Antonia: *King James VI of Scotland, I of England* (Weidenfeld & Nicolson, 1974)

FRASER, Antonia (editor): *Scottish Love Poems* (Canongate, 1975)

GIBBON, Lewis Grassic: *A Scots Quair* (Jarrolds, 1946)

GIBBON, Lewis Grassic and Hugh MACDIARMID: *Scottish Scene or The Intelligent Man's Guide to Albyn* (Hutchinson, 1934)

GIBSON, John S.: *Deacon Brodie: Father to Jekyll and Hyde* (Paul Harris, 1977)

GIFFORD, John, Colin McWILLIAM and David WALKER: *Edinburgh* (The Buildings of Scotland) (Penguin, 1984)

GORDON, Esmé: *The Royal Scottish Academy of Painting, Sculpture & Architecture 1826–1976* (Charles Skilton, 1976)

GORDON, Giles (editor): *Prevailing Spirits: A Book of Scottish Ghost Stories* (Hamish Hamilton, 1976)

GOWANS, James: *Edinburgh and its neighbourhood in the days of our grandfathers* (John C. Nimmo, 1886)

GUNN, Neil M.: *Morning Tide* (Porpoise Press, 1931)

HAINING, Peter (editor): *The Clans of Darkness: Scottish Stories of Fantasy and Horror* (Victor Gollancz, 1971)

HAMILTON, Iain: *Scotland the Brave* (Michael Joseph, 1957)

HOGG, James: *The Private Memoirs and Confessions of a Justified Sinner* (1824)

HUTTON, Laurence: *Literary Landmarks of Edinburgh* (Osgood, McIlvaine, 1891)

IRVINE, Peter: *Scotland the Best! The Essential Guide* (Mainstream, 1995)

JOHNSTON, Thomas: *The History of the Working Classes in Scotland* (Forward Publishing Company, 1921)

KEAY, John and Julia KEAY (editors): *Collins Encyclopaedia of Scotland* (HarperCollins, 1994)

KELMAN, James: *The Busconductor Hines* (Polygon, 1984)

KENNEDY, A. L.: *Night Geometry and the Garscadden Trains* (Polygon, 1990)

LEONARD, Tom (editor): *Radical Renfrew: Poetry from the French Revolution to the First World War* (Polygon, 1990)

LINDSAY, Sir David: *Ane Satyre of the Thrie Estaits*, edited by James Kinsley (Cassell, 1954)

LINKLATER, Eric: *Sealskin Trousers* (Rupert Hart-Davis)

McKEAN, Charles: *The Scottish Thirties: An Architectural Introduction* (Scottish Academic Press, 1987)

MACKENZIE, Compton: *Whisky Galore* (1947)

MACLEAN, Charles and Fritz von der SCHULENBURG: *Romantic Scotland* (Weidenfeld & Nicolson, 1994)

MACLEAN, Sorley: *Collected Poems in Gaelic and English* (Carcanet, 1989)

MACMILLAN, Duncan: *Scottish Art 1460–1990* (Mainstream, 1990)

MACMILLAN, Duncan: *Scottish Art in the 20th Century* (Mainstream, 1994)

McLAREN, Moray (editor): *The Wisdom of the Scots* (Michael Joseph, 1961)

McNEILL, F. Marian: *The Scots Kitchen* (Blackie & Son, 1929)

MACQUEEN, John and Tom SCOTT: *The Oxford Book of Scottish Verse* (Oxford University Press, 1966)

MCWILLIAM, Candia: *Debatable Land* (Bloomsbury, 1994)

MCWILLIAM, Colin: *Lothian except Edinburgh* (The Buildings of Scotland) (Penguin, 1978)

MARTINE, Roddy and Patrick DOUGLAS-HAMILTON: *Scotland: The Land and the Whisky* (John Murray, 1994)

MASSIE, Allan: *100 Great Scots* (Chambers, 1987)

MASSIE, Allan: *Edinburgh* (Sinclair-Stevenson, 1994)

MASSIE, Allan: *Glasgow: Portraits of a City* (Barrie & Jenkins, 1989)

MITCHISON, Rosalind: *A History of Scotland* (Methuen, 1979)

MONCREIFF, Sir Iain: *Simple Heraldry* (Thomas Nelson)

OLIVER, Cordelia: *Joan Eardley, RSA* (Mainstream, 1988)

ROYLE, Trevor (editor): *Jock Tamson's Bairns: Essays on a Scots Childhood* (Hamish Hamilton, 1977)

SCOTT, Sir Walter: *Old Mortality* (1816)

SCOTT, Sir Walter: *The Heart of Midlothian* (1818)

SCOTT, Sir Walter: *Tales of a Grandfather* (1828–30)

SHAKESPEARE, William: *Macbeth*

SMITH, Iain Crichton: *Consider the Lilies* (Victor Gollancz, 1968)

SMITH, Iain Crichton: *Collected Poems* (Carcanet)

SMITH, Sydney Goodsir: *Carotoid Cornucopius* (M. Macdonald, 1964)

SMITH, W. Gordon: *W. G. Gillies: A Very Still Life* (Atelier Books, 1991)

SMOUT, T. C.: *A History of the Scottish People 1560–1830* (Collins, 1969)

SPARK, Muriel: *The Prime of Miss Jean Brodie* (Macmillan, 1961)

SPENCE, Alan: *Its Colours They Are Fine* (Collins, 1977)

STEVENSON, Robert Louis: *The Strange Case of Dr Jekyll and Mr Hyde* (1886)

STEVENSON, Robert Louis: *Kidnapped* (Cassell, 1886)

STEVENSON, Robert Louis: *The Complete Short Stories*, edited by Ian Bell (Mainstream, 1993)

THOMSON, Derick: *An Introduction to Gaelic Poetry* (Victor Gollancz, 1974)

URQUHART, Fred: *The Ploughing Match* (Rupert Hart-Davis, 1968)

URQUHART, Fred and Giles GORDON: *Modern Scottish Short Stories* (Hamish Hamilton, 1978)

WHYTE, Christopher: *Euphemia MacFarrigle and the Laughing Virgin* (Victor Gollancz, 1995)

WILSON, A. N.: *The Laird of Abbotsford: A View of Sir Walter Scott* (Oxford University Press, 1980)

YOUNGSON, A. J.: *The Making of Classical Edinburgh* (Edinburgh University Press, 1966)

Places to Visit

For sites listed here without telephone numbers, please contact Historic Scotland on (0131) 244 3101.

Aberdour Castle
Aberdour, 5m E of Forth Bridge

Ailsa Craig
Island in Firth of Clyde
(01665) 82103

Arbroath Abbey
Arbroath

Ardnamurchan Natural History and
Visitor Centre
2m from Glenborrodale
(0197 24) 254/263

Balmoral Castle
8m W of Ballater
(0133 97) 42334

The Barras
1/4m E of Glasgow Cross, Glasgow
(0141) 552 7258

Beinn Eighe National Nature Reserve
W of A896/A832 junction at Kinlochewe
(0144 584) 258

Borthwick Castle
Off A7, 13m SE of Edinburgh
(01875) 20653

Brodick Castle and Gardens
2m N of Brodick Pier, Isle of Arran
(01770) 2202

The Burrell Collection
Pollok Country Park, Glasgow
(0141) 649 7151

Callanish Standing Stones
12m W of Stornoway, Lewis

Castle Campbell
Dollar Glen, 1m N of Dollar

Castle Menzies
1 1/2m W of Aberfeldy
(01887) 820982

Castle Stalker
Loch Linnhe, 25m NNE of Oban
(0163 173) 234

Castle Urquhart
Loch Ness, 2m SE of Drumnadrochit

Cathedral Church of St Paul
Castlehill, 1 High Street, Dundee
(01382) 202200

Cawdor Castle
Cawdor, between Inverness and Nairn
(0166 77) 615

Culloden Moor
5m E of Inverness
(01463) 790607

Culzean Castle
12m S of Ayr
(0165 56) 274

Dalmeny House
By South Queensferry
(0131) 331 1888

Drum Castle
Drumoak, by Banchory
(01330) 811204

Dryburgh Abbey
6m SE of Melrose

Duart Castle
Off A849, on E point of Mull
(0168 02) 309

Dunnottar Castle
S of Stonehaven
(01569) 62173

Dunrobin Castle
12 1/2m NNE of Dornoch
(01408) 633177

Duns Castle
16m W of Berwick-upon-Tweed
(01361) 83211

Dunstaffnage Castle
4m N of Oban

Edinburgh Castle
Castle Rock, top of Royal Mile

Eilean Donan Castle
9m E of Kyle of Lochalsh
(01599) 85 202

Fair Isle
Between Orkney and Shetland
(0135 12) 258/251

Falls of Glomach
18m E of Kyle of Localsh

Falkland Palace and Gardens
11m N of Kirkcaldy
(0133 757) 397

Fort Augustus Abbey and Fort
S end of Loch Ness, on A82
(01320) 6232

Fort George
B9030, off A96 W of Nairn

Fyvie Castle
8m SE of Turriff
(01651) 891266

Glamis Castle
5m SW of Forfar
(0130 784) 242/243

Glasgow Art Gallery and Museum
Kelvingrove Park, Glasgow
(0141) 357 3929

Glasgow Cathedral
Cathedral Street, Glasgow

Glencoe
17m S of Fort William
(0185 52) 307

Glentress Forest
3m E of Peebles
(01721) 20448

Hopetoun House
W of South Queensferry
(0131) 331 2451

Palace of Holyrood House
Canongate, foot of the Royal Mile,
Edinburgh
(0131) 556 7371/1096

Inveraray Castle
1/2m N of Inveraray
(01499) 2203

Iona
Off SW tip of Mull
(0141) 552 8391

Jedburgh Abbey
High Street, Jedburgh

Kelso Abbey
Bridge Street, Kelso

Linlithgow Palace
S shore of loch, Linlithgow

Melrose Abbey
Main Square, Melrose

National Gallery of Scotland
The Mound, Edinburgh
(0131) 556 8921

Necropolis
Behind Glasgow Cathedral
(0141) 333 0800

Neidpath Castle
1m W of Peebles
(01721) 720333

New Lanark
1m S of Lanark
(01555) 661345

Ruthven Barracks
1/2m S of Kingussie

St Andrews Cathedral
St Andrews

St Giles Cathedral
High Street, Edinburgh
(0131) 225 9442

St Kilda
110m W of Scottish mainland
(0131) 226 5922

Scone Palace
2m NE of Perth
(01738) 52300

Scott Monument
East Princes Street Gardens, Edinburgh
(0131) 225 2424

Scottish National Gallery of Modern Art
Belford Road, Edinburgh
(0131) 556 8921

Skara Brae
19m NW of Kirkwall, Orkney

Stirling Castle
Stirling

Tantallon Castle
3m E of North Berwick

Wallace Monument
Abbey Craig, 1 1/2m NNE of Stirling
(01786) 475019

Index

First published in 1996 by
George Weidenfeld & Nicolson Ltd, The Orion Publishing Group
Orion House, 5, Upper St Martin's Lane, London WC2H 9EA

This edition produced for The Book People Ltd,
Guardian House, Borough Road, Goldalming, Surrey GU7 2AE

A catalogue record for this book is available from the British Library.
ISBN 0–297–83473–8

House editor: Richard Atkinson
Text editor: Clare Currie
Design: The Design Revolution
Map: ML Design
Printed and bound in Italy

The Gordon tartan on the endpaper is from
The Scotch House, 2 Brompton Road, Knightsbridge, London SW1X 7PB.

The photographic images in this book may be obtained
through the Weidenfeld & Nicolson Photographic archive.
Enquiries by telephone (0171) 498 3011 or by fax (0171) 498 0748.
Many other photographs taken from the air by Jason Hawkes are
available from the Jason Hawkes Aerial Collection,
telephone (0171) 486 2800 or fax (01734) 832634.

Photographer's acknowledgements

Firstly, thanks must go to my friend and pilot Tim Kendall, for the many freezing hours we spent flying over Scotland. Also to Jamie, Tanya and Esme for the warm welcome, the message in chalk and the use of their 'car'.

I must of course also mention the publishers of this book, specifically Anthony Cheetham, Michael Dover and my editor Richard Atkinson; thank you for all your help and commitment.

Jason Hawkes, January 1996

Author's acknowledgements

I am grateful to Tommy and Rose Maley for driving around the streets of Glasgow and identifying the tower blocks on page 36; to Bridget McKernan, John and Elaine McKernan, and Norman and Clare McNiven for instructing me, Edinburgh born and bred, on the complexities of Glasgow; and to my wife, Maggie McKernan, for generally keeping me going at a time of personal difficulty.

I am particularly grateful to my secretary and assistant, Jane Darling, without whose input and ordering of the photographs the text of this book would not have seen the light of day.

Dave Goffin of the Red Deer Commission in his own time provided an elegant account of deer in Scotland; space only permitted me to use a tithe of it. Fiona Watts of the Scottish Office Central Statistic Unit directed me to statistical information on the geography of Scotland. Iain Crichton Smith kindly allowed me to quote lines from his luminous poem, 'Deer on the High Hills', and Magnus Linklater from his article in *The Times* dated 16 October 1995 about the Skye road bridge.

It was generous, if not foolhardy, of Michael Dover, publisher of illustrated books at Weidenfeld & Nicolson, to invite me to write the text. My editor, Richard Atkinson, has been a model of what an editor should be.

Giles Gordon, January 1996